Communion

100 Days Of Intimacy With The WORD

A **GRACE** DAILY DEVOTIONAL

Communion

100 Days Of Intimacy With The WORD

CHARIS**RESOURCES**

XULON PRESS

Xulon Press
2301 Lucien Way #415
Maitland, FL 32751
407.339.4217
www.xulonpress.com

Printed in the United States of America.

ISBN-13: 978-1-6628-1242-2

Dedicated to all the partners and residents of GHC
Thank you for your relentless participation
in God's divine mandate in your sphere of influence
The best is yet to come

Communion

Topical Outline

devotion

Be devoted to not only the studying of the Word
but to the doing of the Word

Communion

GIVING THE WORD FIRST PLACE

But the Lord answered and said to her, "Martha, Martha, you are worried and bothered about so many things; but only one thing is necessary, for Mary has chosen the good part, which shall not be taken away from her." (Luke 10:41-42 NASB)

Giving the word first place is the key to a vibrant and successful life. This is something that many of God's people do not know whose lives don't reflect the glow of the Spirit. Their attitude towards the things of God is a revelation that they have not given the word of God His first place in their lives. Listen saint, there is no life outside of the word of God. Hear me! Anything outside the word of God has death programmed in it. Romans 8:6 (NIV) says "The mind governed by the flesh is death..." in other words, anyone whose words, actions and inactions are governed by things other than the word of God will end in ruins. A marriage, business, job, relationship that is not rooted in the word of God will end in ruins. When I say "rooted in the word of God," I am talking about an unqualified and irrevocable committal to God and His Word.

Jesus said in Matthew 7:24-27 (ESV) "Everyone then who hears these words of mine and does them will be like a wise man who built his house on the rock. And the rain fell, and the floods came, and the winds blew and beat on that house, but it did not fall, because it had been founded on the rock. And everyone who hears these words of mine and does not do them will be like a foolish man who built his house on the sand. And the rain fell, and the floods came, and the winds blew and beat against that house, and it fell, and great was the fall of it." The contrast here is that the wise man whose house was built on the rock, gave the word first place. The foolish man on the other hand was just a mere hearer. Jesus said when the conflict of life sprang up, great was the fall of that house, marriage, business etc.

Think about this for a moment; Jesus came into the house of Martha and Mary. The appropriate thing would have been that both sisters saw to the welfare of their guest and made sure that He was comfortable and well served. By the way, this guest was Jesus. Martha did what was appropriate in the eyes of men. Frustrated about the fact that Jesus allowed her sister to act like she was not properly raised, after all, if anybody should know, it should be Jesus. Then Martha - in Luke 10:40 MSG - stepped in, interrupting them. And said "Master, don't you care that my sister has abandoned the kitchen to me? Tell her to lend me a hand." Then Jesus said the unthinkable. "Martha, Martha, you are worried and bothered about so many things; but only one thing is necessary, for Mary has chosen the good part, which shall not be taken away from her." Luke 10:41-42 (NASB)

Maybe your excuse is "I have three jobs and three children to take care of" or "I have a lot of bills to settle. Hence, I don't have time to attend church right now." "Oh, besides, my daughter's soccer practice is on Sundays." I would commit to the things of God if it were not for these things. God understands." Jesus said to Martha, ONE THING IS NEEDFUL- THE DOING OF THE WORD.

So, what do I do? GIVE GOD FIRST PLACE IN YOUR LIFE. Give the word of God first place. Get committed at church. Where is God on your calendar? Make the necessary adjustments. Let your daily schedule reflect that you are born again. Do not accept any appointments that will infringe on your commitment to God. Praise God!

Faith-Filled Confession:
The Word of God is my light, life, victory and reality. I give priority to the Word in everything today. I open my soul to the ministry of God's Word today. I refuse to observe or give attention to anything that does not accord to the Word of God in my life today. In the name of the Lord Jesus Christ.

STUDY FOR YOURSELF

"Do not be carried away by all kinds of strange teachings, for it is good for the heart to be strengthened by grace and not by ceremonial foods, which are of no value to those devoted to them." (Hebrews 13:9 NIV)

There are a lot of God's people experiencing difficulties in just about every area of their lives, and as a result, life has become a mystery to them. And it appears as though their unsaved colleagues are getting ahead while they continue to struggle. They have prayed every prayer, yet it appears as though the heavens are closed over them. Then they hear statements like, "A Christian is an absolute victor over sickness, lack, and the world," and it rattles their theology because they have classified such teaching as religion or false. They think because they are having a hard time getting by in life that everyone else is experiencing the same; so, they gravitate towards people who have their kind of experiences. Listen, you don't need to be in church to have someone agree with you about your struggles. I bet if you listened hard enough you would hear people on the street say that they are struggling too. It may sound nice and spiritual, but at the end of the day, the question that you must answer is this: "What does the Word say?"

After Paul had that glorious encounter with Jesus that led to his salvation and call into the ministry, the Scriptures declare that he "...immediately preached Christ in the synagogues, that He is the Son of God." In other words, he proclaimed the message of Christ and all that the believer is (authority, identity and ability) in Christ. The Apostle Paul put it this way in 2 Corinthians 4:5 (NLT), "You see, we don't go around preaching about ourselves. We preach that Jesus Christ is Lord, and we ourselves are your servants for Jesus' sake." The Apostle could have gone around preaching his experience (which was subject to change) and not the gospel of the kingdom.

Saint, the quality of our life is a function of your revelation; the more you know what belongs to you in the kingdom, the better the quality of your life here on earth. Jesus said, "and you will know the truth, and the truth will make you free." (John 8:32 NLT) Truth here is not relative as some have suggested. Bible Truth is absolute!

Sadly, many live their lives based on "religious facts or relative truth" masquerading as truth and in many instances, have replaced Truth with human sentiments. Fact says that you are in pain and struggling, but truth declares you are victorious and healed. Fact says that you are miserable, but truth declares you are glorious. Fact says that you are broke, but truth says you are rich. Fact says that you are not perfect, but the truth says you are perfect in Christ Jesus. Fact says we're all sinners, but truth says you are the righteousness of God. As believers, we are to live by the Truth and not by facts. All that we do should be from the place of truth. Our confessions and mannerisms should always stem from the Word of God; from a position of triumph and victory in Christ knowing that everything that Jesus died for us to have is irreversible. I want to encourage and admonish that you study the Bible for yourself; it would help you to lay hold of all that is yours in Christ Jesus.

Faith-Filled Confession:
I stand defenseless to the Word of God. I let go of old wives' fables. I refuse to judge the Word by my experiences or by the experiences of others. I endorse the truth of God's word in every area of my life. I say let God be true and every circumstance or thing that does not glorify Christ be a lie!

ENJOY HIS PRESENCE

"Did not our hearts burn within us, while He talked with us by the way, and while He opened to us the Scriptures?" (Luke 24:32 KJV)

There are so many things that Satan can fake; he may fake signs, healings, and miracles. However, there is one thing that He will never be able to fake and that is the true presence of God. David said in Psalm 16:11 (KJV), "Thou wilt shew me the path of life: in thy presence is fullness of joy; at thy right hand there are pleasures forevermore." The presence of God brings such joy and peace that may not necessarily correlate with our circumstances. The people of the world may look at you and wonder why you are smiling; they may wonder how you are able to laugh, rejoice, and still praise God in the midst of what they see as trouble. For the Christian, this is only possible because of the presence of God. His abiding presence in our hearts and the comfort we receive from His Word unlocks in us, peace, joy, and strength.

After Jesus' resurrection, He spent time with some of His disciples eating with them and studying the Scriptures with them, and after He had left, they said amongst themselves, "Did not our hearts burn within us, while He talked with us by the way, and while He opened to us the Scriptures?" (Luke 24:32 KJV) The burn that they felt within them was a manifestation of God's presence. There is something special about the manifest presence of God. No wonder Peter said at the Mount of Transfiguration, "Lord, it's wonderful for us to be here! If you want, I'll make three shelters as memorials— one for you, one for Moses, and one for Elijah." (Matthew 17:4 NLT) Moses so desired the presence of God that he said in Exodus 33:15 (NIV), "If Your presence does not go with us, do not send us up from here." The presence of God makes all the difference! Unlike in the day of Moses when the presence of God came and left, the Christian today houses the presence of God. Jesus said, "...behold, I am with you always, to the end of the age." (Matthew 28:20 ESV) And you may not always physically feel the presence of God, but you should always know that He is with you and you can always access His presence through His Word. So, set your heart on His Word today and retain in your mind a consciousness of His presence in you and with you. It is this consciousness that gives you a Christ-confidence; such that made Paul the Apostle say in Philippians 4:13 (NKJV), "I can do all things through Christ who strengthens me.". As you become more acquainted with the Lord through the acknowledging of His presence in your life from day to day, you will become increasingly Christ-confident to the point where you will know in your heart that ANYTHING IS POSSIBLE.

Faith-Filled Confession:
II am assured of the presence of my Father, for God has said that He would never leave me nor forsake me. So, no matter the situation, I know that I have already prevailed in Christ Jesus. I am victorious. I see all things working together for my good. Hallelujah!

BE RECEPTIVE TO THE WORD

"Your testimonies have I taken as a heritage forever: for they are the rejoicing of my heart." (Psalm 119:111 KJV)

You are the manifestation of the counsel of God,

the dream of the Father in action, a living and walking Word of God. You are a special craftsmanship of the Father. Everything about you is supernatural.

In Psalms 119:111, David was saying. "I have taken the word hostage forever: for they are my source of joy." He made a great discovery about the Word and he got excited about it. You too can be this excited about the Word of God. The Contemporary English Version of the Bible reads: "They will always be my most prized possession and my source of joy."

The Word of God is a maker of what it talks about. It is a conveyor of divinity. Sometimes you hear people say "this and that happened to me." Brother! Sister! To us, only the word of God happens to us! No wonder John cried out, in 1 John 1:1-2 (KJV), "that which was from the beginning, which we have heard, which we have seen with our eyes, which we have looked upon, and our hands have handled, of the Word of life." He went further and declared that it "...was manifested unto us." Glory!

You are an offspring of the same Word of Life. Therefore, your life is a beautiful place; a showroom that displays heaven's glory. Don't talk depression and frustration like others! You are different! Be authentic! You have a Word life! You are the change that others are hoping for, a dispenser of the grace of God. You are God's potent material for change in your family, on the job and in the community. Wake up to your reality in Christ. Glory to God!

In Acts 17:11 (NIV), the Bible declares "The people of Berea were more noble than the people of Thessalonica. They were very willing to receive God's message, and every day they carefully examined the Scriptures to see if what Paul said was true." Did you notice that it is noble to be receptive to the word of God?

Not only did they attend church, but they also gave audience and attention to the Word of God. It does presuppose that they had their Bibles and writing materials with them. How do you know? You may ask. Because the scripture says, "...they were very willing to receive God's message, and every day they carefully examined the Scriptures to see if what Paul said was true." They were not going to take the word of the preacher for it, they studied and examined the Word of God for themselves.

You may already be thinking, "Pastor, I have tried in the past to study the Word but I always fall asleep whenever I do." Or, "I really don't have any desire to study; I don't think it is for me. Maybe it is for those that are spiritual nuts." To think and accept such thinking is like putting your finger on a hot stove and hoping it will not hurt you. May I remind you that many of us started that way, but the deep in us kept crying out for the depth in God. Your confession is so vital at this stage. You may not feel that desire, but you have to keep confessing, "my spirit longs for the Word of God and I am enabled to receive from God's word." A little discipline will be needed. But just keep pressing; don't accept your lack of receptiveness for the Word. Use your confession of the Word to compel your feelings to line up with the Word of God.

I will encourage you to pray Ephesians 3:16-19 and Colossians 1:9-11

Faith-Filled Confession:
I refuse to stagger, vacillate or look away from the reality of the Word of God. The Word of God in me does not fail. Therefore, I yield to God's instructions concerning me today. No matter what I see, feel or hear. The Word of stand supreme in my life. I rejoice knowing that the Word is living and active in all my endeavors in Jesus' name.

STUFF YOUR MIND WITH THE WORD

"Guard your heart above all else, for it determines the course of your life." (Proverbs 4:23 NLT)

This may be the most important thing you hear this year, as a matter of fact, this will determine the outcome of your life experience, finance, family, career or business. Guarding your heart is something that God will not do for you or anyone else for that matter. It is your solemn responsibility. I have seen so many people, beautiful, young and strong fall off the "cliff of life" because of the failure to guard that precious component of their life – THE MIND.

Failure is a function of the mind; not resources. You have to hear me, please. No man was born a failure. You may have been born in the worst circumstance imaginable, but you were not born a failure. Failure is a choice, just like success is a choice. The Message translation of Proverbs 4:23 reads, "keep vigilant, watch over your heart; that's where life starts." The NLT says "for it determines the course of your life". Meaning, your mind is a "YOKE MACHINE," that can program you for either success or failure. Genesis 11:6 (KJV) says, "...and now nothing will be restrained from them, which they have imagined to do." There is a latent power that the mind possesses, that defiles impossibility. What you feed the mind is what the mind will produce for you in an excellent fashion – failure or success. For this reason, you must guard your heart above all else.

What most people do not know is that it is easier to succeed than it's to fail. Most people may not agree, but it's true. As a child of God, success is in your spirit. You are a reproduction of success. This is the reason we must preach the gospel and tell everyone about the power of salvation.

So, how do I guard my heart as a child of God? Stuff it with the word of God! Season your thoughts with the word! Saturate your mind with God's word, until there is an outpouring. Hallelujah!! When you stuff your mind with the word, expect an avalanche of what it talks about. Joshua 1:8 (NLT) says "... you will be prosperous and successful in everything." Imagine stuffing a powerful machine called the mind with materials loaded with creative ability – The Word. I can tell you the result - PERMANENT SUCCESS AND PROSPERITY.

The beautiful thing is that where there is fullness, there is an outpouring. When your heart is fully stuffed with the Word, there will be an outpouring of the word, and that's where you are changed and promoted to greater heights in all that you do. Choose what you consume. Consume contents that promote righteousness. Study your Bible for yourself. Stuff your mind to the full till there is no room for doubt and unbelief or anything negative. When contrary thoughts and images surface in your mind, contest it with the word; cast it down with your faith declaration. Jesus said, "...what you say flows from what is in your heart." (Luke 6:45 NLT) Then He said in Mark 11:23 "...you shall have whatsoever you say and continue to say." Proverbs 13:3 (CJB) "He who guards his mouth preserves his life, but one who talks too much comes to ruin."

Stuff your heart with God's word today, for it determines the course of your life.

Faith-Filled Confession:
My mind is set on an irreversible and unstoppable path of victory and success by the Holy Ghost. I fix my gaze on the Word only today. Lord, you have my attention today. It's my honor to see you work wonders in and through me today. Have your way today in Jesus' name.

LOOK AT THE MIRROR

But we all, with unveiled face, beholding as in a mirror the glory of the Lord, are being transformed into the same image from glory to glory, just as from the Lord, the Spirit. (2 Corinthians 3:18 KJV)

The way some Christians talk and act, it almost

appears as though God showed favor to some of us and others were not so lucky. Life is not a lottery. It is not subject to time and chance. Life is eternal, meaning, it is spiritual. It responds only to understanding. Solomon said, "Wisdom is the principal thing; therefore, get wisdom: and with all thy getting get understanding." (Proverbs 4:7 KJV) The quality of your life is squarely your responsibility. It is dependent on how much of God's Word you have appropriated with understanding. A Christian will not be delivered irrespective of their tears or fasting and prayers. All that will not amount to anything before God. The reason being, they are trying to get God to do something that He already did. Better still, they are trying to get God to see something that does not exist.

Failure is unnecessary as a child of God. A Christian does not have any business failing in life. How is failure even possible with a Christian? Failure is foreign when you walk in the reality of Christ. I am talking about walking in absolute success and victory every day. Listen! This is who you are: When you were born again, you were born a victor and a success, and that hasn't changed. You are still a victor and a success like you were when you made Jesus the Lord of your life. You are a message from God; your very smile is a message of prosperity. Every step you take is God's handwriting. Don't walk and talk like you don't mean anything. No! Do not talk like the rest of the world. You are different. You have the Life and the nature of God in you. You are someone very special. Glory to God!

The mirror is a beautification tool and so is the Word of God. It is given to you so that you can beautify your divine life. Imagine someone telling you that you have a blemish on your forehead and you check it out for yourself using a mirror and find no blemish.

My question is this: which report will you believe? It is the same thing with the Word of God. The Word of God is the mirror - the mirror of reality. I am encouraging you to learn to see yourself in the light of God's Word in Christ Jesus. See yourself in the finished work of Christ. Accept that what Jesus did is final and live every day with that consciousness.

2 Corinthians 3:18 (KJV) "...we all with unveiled face, beholding as in a mirror the glory of the Lord, are being transformed into the same image from glory to glory..." Meaning, whenever you meditate on the Word of God, you are transported from one level of glory to another. Hallelujah!

The secret to a life of ever-increasing glory is to stand in front of the mirror of God which is the Word and confess again and again whatever you see in the mirror. Begin to meditate on the Word of God today. Listen to the podcast and let it saturate your thoughts. Confess out loud the faith-filled confessions and it will bring you into a greater glory. A presentation of the divine you! The invincible you to your world. Praise God!

Faith-Filled Confession:
Father in the name of Jesus, I thank you that your eternal word is unchanging. My victory is eternal. Christ's abiding victory is my victory. I am conscious of my victory, success and prosperity. Praise God!

CONSCIOUSNESS BREEDS CONFESSION

"You are my King and my God. You command victories for Israel. Only by your power can we push back our enemies; only in your name can we trample our foes. I do not trust in my bow; I do not count on my sword to save me. You are the one who gives us victory over our enemies; you disgrace those who hate us. O God, we give glory to you all day long and constantly praise your name." (Psalm 44:4-8 NLT)

There are no accidental successes or failures. Even if you were born into a disadvantaged situation by your parents, the responsibility is ultimately yours to define your future. And if you are going to define your future to be an exhibition of the grace and power of God, then you must understand the law of recognition. Recognition is an acknowledgment that conveys approval or sanction. It's the law that brings you into fellowship or oneness with what you are recognizing. It's the law that creates realities and your reality governs your everyday life. Look at David for example, you can tell where his heart was. You can see what constituted his imaginations. You can see what his reality was when it came to the battles he fought. His attitude consistently expressed his trust in the presence of God that was with him. His recognition of the presence of God was profound and we see this all through his psalms. He said, "You are my King and my God. You command victories for Israel. Only by your power can we push back our enemies; only in your name can we trample our foes. I do not trust in my bow; I do not count on my sword to save me. You are the one who gives us victory over our enemies; you disgrace those who hate us. O God, we give glory to you all day long and constantly praise your name." (Psalm 44:4-8 NLT)

Even as a young lad, he said to King Saul after recounting how he slew a bear and a lion, in his attempt to get the King to send him to take down Goliath, David said, "The Lord who rescued me from the paw of the lion and the paw of the bear will rescue me from the hand of this Philistine." (1 Samuel 17:37 NIV) Then when he finally got the green light to fight against Goliath, he said to the

15

Philistine, "Thou comest to me with a sword, and with a spear, and with a shield: but I come to thee in the name of the Lord of hosts, the God of the armies of Israel, whom thou hast defied." (1 Samuel 17:45 KJV) Did you notice how he consistently confessed to the Lord? You can tell that his confidence was rooted in his reality that God was with him. No wonder God testified concerning him: "I have found David son of Jesse, a man after my own heart; he will do everything I want him to do." (Acts 13:22 NIV)

In Hebrews 6:12, we are admonished to not become half-hearted but to be imitators of those who through faith and patient endurance are now heirs to the promises. And I believe David was one of those spoken of. He lived his whole life on this simple truth: Recognition and proclamation of God's divine ability. He constantly affirmed the goodness and sovereignty of the Almighty God who is faithful to His Words. Look at Jesus, He was recognition and proclamation personified. His consciousness of the Father was unbelievable! At one time, He said, "...whoever has seen me has seen the Father...." (John 14:9 ESV) What a confession!

As new creations in Christ, this must become the hallmark of our everyday lives. We must maintain a consciousness of the spiritual. We must recognize that we are not alone. And this consciousness will utter our communication and our communication will create our reality which will ultimately govern our everyday lives. Praise God!

Faith-Filled Confession:
Father God in the name of Jesus, I boldly confess that as You are, so am I in this world. Therefore, in my path, there is no financial, mental or emotional disability. The joy of the Lord is my strength today. I am conscious of Father God, of the divine presence of the Holy Ghost. I yield my mind and body to His promptings today. I declare that the name of Jesus is glorified in me today. In the name of the Lord Jesus. Praise God!

EAT THE WORD

"When your words came, I ate them; they were my joy and my heart's delight, for I bear your name, Lord God Almighty." (Jeremiah 15:16 NIV)

It is important what you are feeding on. We hear time and time again how important it is to pay attention to what we feed our physical bodies because of the health benefits from certain foods and the health risks posed by others. But did you know that it is even more important what you feed your spirit? Oh yes, the spirit needs to be nourished too and if all you do is feed your body and neglect your spirit, you will experience spiritual malnutrition which the Bible refers to as "being carnal." And Romans 8:6 tells us that being carnally minded is death. In other words, if all you are concerned about is pleasuring your flesh at the expense of your spirit, you have set death in motion. On the other hand, if you invest in the nourishment of your spirit, you are guaranteed to experience life and peace.

Jesus came to make it possible for you to not only have life but also enjoy it (John 10:10). He did more than die for your sins. His life, death, burial and resurrection were also for your health, wealth, peace, joy, wholeness and prosperity. 1 John 1:2 (KJV) declares, "Beloved, I wish above all things that thou mayest prosper and be in health, even as thy soul prospereth." The will of God is the word of God and the will of God concerning your life has already been established. His will has always been for you to have a rich, enjoyable and satisfying life; not when you get to heaven, but here on earth. Though His will is established, His will is not automatic. His established will needs your co-operation. 2 Peter 3:9 tells us that God's will is for everyone to be saved and for all to come to repentance. Though this is an established will of God, it is not automatic because we know that not all will accept Jesus. In the same vein, just as God's will and plan is for you to enjoy life, it will not happen automatically. You must play your part.

Jeremiah by the inspiration of the Holy Spirit said, "When Your words came, I ate them; they were my joy and my heart's delight, for I bear your name, Lord God Almighty" (Jeremiah 15:16 NIV) Jeremiah had an understanding of what the Word does. He said He ate the Word of God. And when he ate and digested the word of God, the word began to produce joy and a delightful heart. He fed on the word until the Word began to produce. Hallelujah! What is your attitude to the word of God? Have you been eating word? Has it been producing fruit for you?

God told Joshua; "This Book of the Law shall not depart from your mouth, but you shall meditate in it day and night, that you may observe to do according to all that is written in it. For then you will make your way prosperous, and then you will have good success. "The Good News Translation says, "Never stop reciting these teachings. You must think about them night and day so that you will faithfully do everything written in them. Only then will you prosper and succeed." (Joshua 1:8 GNT) In other words, don't stop talking His word, regardless of what you see, feel or hear. Find rest, joy and peace in God's Word. When the Word of God comes to you, respond with joy! The Psalmist said, "I rejoice at thy word, as one that findeth great spoil." (Psalm 119:162 KJV. And when you get a hold of the Word of God, do not stop declaring it!

Faith-Filled Confession:
Father, I thank You for Your word that declares that I am healed. I thank You that I am a success. I thank You that no weapon that is formed or fashioned against me prospers. I thank You that this is my year of the Exceeding Grace. Thank You for uncommon miracles. I testify of Your greatness and goodness. In Jesus' name!

Faith-Filled Confession:
Father, I thank You for Your word that declares that I am healed. I thank You that I am a success. I thank You that no weapon that is formed or fashioned against me prospers. I thank You that this is my year of the Exceeding Grace. Thank You for uncommon miracles. I testify of Your greatness and goodness. In Jesus' name! Hallelujah! Glory!

discipleship

After Jesus' resurrection, He spent time with some
of His disciples eating with them and studying the
Scriptures with them

Communion

SERVING GOD THE RIGHT WAY

"First, I thank my God through Jesus Christ for you all, that your faith is spoken of throughout the whole world. For God is my witness, whom I serve with my spirit in the gospel of his Son, that without ceasing I make mention of you always in my prayers." (Romans 1:8-9 KJV)

As a young Christian, there was a song I sang,

again, and again as I cried out my heart. The song goes, "Lord, I want to be like Jesus in my heart." We sang this song expressing our desires of wanting to walk like Jesus, speak like Jesus, and ultimately perform the miracles that He performed. Simply put, we wanted to serve God like Jesus served the Father. However, as I look back today, I am forced to wonder how we maintained such mindsets, and where our Bibles where because it is obvious that we didn't see Scriptures such as John 14:12, 1 John 4:17 and Acts 1:8. The things we cried out to God for were the very things He anointed us for. No wonder, we were a bunch of ineffective Christians who thought that our cries would make up for our spiritual bankruptcies especially in the area of soul winning.

Up till this day, you would hardly find a Christian who does not have a desire to serve God. We all want to serve God, but the question remains, "How do I serve God in a way that is pleasing to Him?" The answer is simple. To do so, we must focus on the most pressing thing on the heart of God and 1 Timothy 2:4 (KJV) tells us what that is. It says that God desires "...to have all men saved, and to come unto the knowledge of the truth." The Father's most pressing desire right now is soul-winning and discipleship. So, if your desire is to serve God, I would encourage you to work on winning those within your sphere of influence for Jesus Christ.

However, in doing so, you must remember that the Holy Spirit is behind every soul that is won. Our job is simply to be the speaker. It's not in our own strength that people receive salvation or accept our invitations to attend church, it's all the work of the Holy Spirit. Jesus said in John 20:21 (DBT), "...Peace to you. As the Father has sent Me forth, I also send you." In other words, the same mandate and power of the Holy Spirit that was on Jesus, He has placed on you for your family, friends, co-workers, neighbors, and all that God will bring your way. Sometimes, all you must do is to invite them to church or sow a seed of kindness into their lives. Don't be afraid to say, "I would love for you to come to church with me." That simple invitation can be the catalyst that will ultimately bring them to the saving knowledge of Jesus Christ. And from my experience, many who accept the invitation to go to church first were ministered to by the one that invited them to church.

Service to God which is demonstrated in soul-winning can take many forms. However, our goal must be to reach someone with the Good News of Jesus Christ. So, be the one that touches the heart of the Father by making an investment in the lives of those that do not believe in Jesus.

Faith-Filled Confession:
As the deer pants for the water brooks, so pants my soul for You, O God. You, my God, are my source, strength, and sustainer. I choose to serve You with my whole being and with all that I have. Today, I declare that as for me and my household, we shall serve the Lord. Amen!

SERVING IN THE GOSPEL IS YOUR OBLIGATION

"For if I preach the gospel, I have nothing to boast of, for necessity is laid upon me; yes, woe is me if I do not preach the gospel!" (1 Corinthians 9:16 NKJV)

There is a new trend that I have come to notice among many of my brothers and sisters in Christ. It is what I call Christianity based on convenience. And it says, "I serve God when I think I can, and when I think I can't, I don't." It's the mindset that I will do my part when I have done everything else. Serving God has almost become a hobby; something that we do when we have room in our schedules. Some people even devote more time to their hobbies than they do their service to God. Child of God, it ought not to be so. God ought to always be in first place. You do not do kingdom work during your free time. On the contrary, you should schedule other activities around it, and as much as is possible, include it in other activities. There should be a sense of responsibility and a sense of obligation when it comes to our service to God and our commitment to our assignment. We all have the ministry of preaching the gospel and that this ministry is divided into two parts—our personal ministry to share the gospel with those around us, and our ministry to fulfill our assignments in our local church. And when it comes to fulfilling our ministry, it should be with a sense of obligation.

In 1 Corinthians 9:16 (NKJV), Apostle Paul said, "...necessity is laid upon me; yes, woe is me if I do not preach the gospel!" Apostle Paul understood his responsibility and obligation. To the point that he said, "if I do not do my part, it is to my grief and distress." He said, "woe is me." How many have that mindset today? Too many today think that if they do not do their part that someone else will. The sense of obligation has become foreign. It's almost like we think there will always be someone else to pick up the slack or that God will understand when we are being ineffective. But here is the truth— NO EXCUSE IS GOOD ENOUGH. In Luke 9 (NKJV), Jesus called a man to follow Him and the man said to Jesus, "... Lord, let me first go and bury my father." (vs 59) And Jesus said to the man, "Let the dead bury their own dead, but you go and preach the kingdom of God." (vs 60) What was Jesus saying here? He was simply saying, "Let nothing stand in the way of you doing what God has called you to do."

In 1 Corinthians 9:17 (NKJV), Apostle Paul continued, "For if I do this [preach the gospel] willingly, I have a reward; but if against my will, I have been entrusted with a stewardship." What a mindset to have! Apostle Paul was saying, "Look, I don't have a choice in this matter. This is not about the gains. This is not something that I do just because I am bored and need something to do. This is something that I MUST do because I have been entrusted with a stewardship." Now, we can see why his ministry was full of results. He was not a fair-weather Christian. He understood stewardship and obligation.

Like the Apostle Paul, we have been entrusted with a stewardship, and necessity is laid on us to our parts. So, do not wait for the praise or encouragement of men to do what God has called you to do. Be faithful and allow God Himself to reward you.

Faith-Filled Confession:
The Lord God is my sun and shield; He has risen upon me and His rays bring me health, wholeness, and freedom. The Lord gives me grace and glory; no good thing has He withheld from me. He has made my life a theater for the miraculous. Hallelujah! (Malachi 4:2; Psalm 84:11)

SERVE ACCORDING TO PRESCRIBED ORDER

"For God is my witness, whom I serve with my spirit in the gospel of His Son, that without ceasing I make mention of you always in my prayers." (Romans 1:9 KJV)

There is a prescribed way to serve God, and we

must be aware of this as believers. "As long as it gets done, or as long as I make an effort." is not enough. This was Cain's attitude in his service to God; the attitude of, "Oh! He better be glad I gave an offering." No honey, it is not about your offering. There is a prescribed way to give an offering. Cain failed to follow the prescribed way and his offering was rejected by God (Genesis 4:5-7). Brethren, it is not about what we do for God. The question is this: Did you follow the prescribed way? Did you do it with the right attitude?

In John 4:24 (KJV) Jesus tells us, "God is a Spirit: and they that worship Him must worship Him in spirit and in truth." Meaning, true worship that is acceptable to God must come from our spirit and must be according to the Word. So many rely on their human strength in their service to God, no wonder they get easily frustrated and discouraged when they do not see the desired results. This applies not only in the things we do in the house of God but in every area of our lives. In Ephesians 6:7 and Colossians 3:23, we are admonished to do everything wholeheartedly as unto the Lord. 1 Samuel 2:9 tells us that no man prevails by human strength. Listen, signs of frustration are signs that one who has taken their gaze off God and His Word and are relying on their own ability.

Romans 1:9 (KJV) says, "For God is my witness, whom I serve with my spirit in the gospel of His Son..." In other words, Paul ensured that His service to God was not from his flesh but from his spirit. He understood that the flesh never has anything good to offer. You may ask, "How can I ensure that my service to God is with my spirit?" It is simple. You serve God with your spirit by doing His Word; by following His instructions. Let's use the giving of tithe as an example. When it comes to giving your tithe, it has to be done according to God's prescribed order. The Bible says in Malachi 3:10 (NIV), "Bring the whole tithe into the storehouse, that there may be food in My house. Test me in this,' says the Lord Almighty, 'and see if I will not throw open the floodgates of heaven and pour out so much blessing that there will not be room enough to store it."' You cannot then give your tithe to the poor or help out a family member to pay their rent and say that you gave your tithe to God. The instruction was to bring the whole tithe into the storehouse which is your local church. Is it then wrong to help the poor or a family member in need? Certainly not! God wants you to do those things but not with your tithe. If you do not follow the prescribed order, do not expect to receive the blessing. The blessing is attached to the instruction. In the twentieth chapter of the Book of Numbers, we see a frustrated Moses. God asked him to speak to the rock so that God's people and their livestock would have water to drink. Out of frustration from the complaints of the people, rather than speak to the rock as he was instructed, Moses struck the rock twice and still, water came out as God had desired. But the problem was that he did not follow the prescribed order. For that, He missed out on God's best.

Apostle Paul by the Holy Ghost said to Timothy, "So you, my son, be strong [constantly strengthened] and empowered in the grace that is [to be found only] in Christ Jesus." (2 Timothy 2:1 AMP) In other words, take advantage of the grace that is in Christ Jesus; do not rely on your human abilities. Anchor yourself on God and His Word and rely on His strength in all that you do. On your job, in your home, in your education, in whatever it is that you do, take advantage of Grace.

Faith-Filled Confession:
I can do all things through Christ who strengthens me. I am self-sufficient in Christ's sufficiency. I anchor myself on the eternal and unfailing Word of God. I refuse to rely on the flesh; I function by the Spirit in all that I do. I choose to take advantage of Grace. In Jesus' name. Amen.

SERVE FROM YOUR SPIRIT

"For God is my witness, whom I serve with my spirit in the gospel of his Son, that without ceasing I make mention of you always in my prayers." (Romans 1:9 KJV)

Jesus said in John 4:23 (NLT), "But the time is coming—indeed it's here now—when true worshipers will worship the Father in spirit and in truth. The Father is looking for those who will worship Him that way." The word "worship" in this verse could also mean serve or service. Hence, this verse can also read "The Father is looking for those who will serve Him in spirit and in truth." Notice that God is particular about the quality of service He receives; He said it must be done in Spirit and in Truth. This means that our service to God must carry the touch of Heaven. It must be selfless and from a heart that is full of the love of God. And when it comes to serving God, it's all about winning others to Jesus Christ. I'll ask you, "Does your worship help others encounter God?" If it doesn't, then, it is in vain because worship that is offered in Spirit and in Truth is designed to draw people to Jesus. And worship is not all about singing songs; worship is ministering to the heart of God. It's being deliberate about meeting the desires of God in the earth and 1 Timothy 2:4 spells out His divine desire — soul-winning and discipleship.

When Paul the Apostle said in Romans 1:9 (KJV), "For God is my witness, whom I serve with my spirit in the gospel of His Son, that without ceasing I make mention of you always in my prayers." He was saying in essence, that his worship to God was demonstrated in his preaching of the gospel. The New Living Translation puts it this way: "God knows how often I pray for you. Day and night, I bring you and your needs in prayer to God, whom I serve with all my heart by spreading the Good News about His Son." In other words, by serving the needs of others, he was ministering to the heart of God and the quality of his service was as though he was physically attending to Jesus; not with the notion that he was doing the people a favor. Colossians 3:23-24 (KJV) says, "And whatsoever ye do, do it heartily, as to the Lord, and not unto men; knowing that of the Lord ye shall receive the reward of the inheritance: for ye serve the Lord Christ."

Ministering to the heart of God begins with you looking out for a human need and meeting it, and man's number one need is a Savior—Jesus Christ. To do this, you don't have to look far. Just look at those whom you call friends or family. Begin by serving them like you would Jesus. Share the gospel with them; find a way to minister to their needs and in doing that, Jesus will receive the glory.

Faith-Filled Confession:
Father, in the name of the Lord Jesus, open my eyes to see opportunities where I can serve You with the strength, I have received from You. Use me to pray for others, to bear their burdens, to encourage them and to help them. Administer Your love and grace through me, in Jesus' name, Amen.

TRUE SERVICE WILL COST YOU

"Then Jesus said to His disciples, "Whoever wants to be my disciple must deny themselves and take up their cross and follow Me." (Matthew 16:24 NIV)

The Scripture tells us of a fellow who said to Jesus,

"I will follow you wherever you go." (Luke 9:57 ESV) Oftentimes, we hear people make similar statements, "Lord, I will do whatever you want me to do" and thirty minutes after saying that, they are walking in offense; offended that their pastor corrected them; offended at their spouse over trivial issues. When this fellow said to Jesus, "I will follow You wherever you go," Jesus knew right away that his heart was in the wrong place. This fellow was only interested in the fame that came with being Jesus' disciple but had no desire for the process of discipleship. Just like so many today who want to be popular without giving themselves to the process of discipleship and stewardship. Jesus said to him, "Foxes have dens and birds have nests, but the Son of Man has no place to lay his head." (Luke 9:58 NIV) In simple terms, Jesus was saying, "If you are looking for overnight fame, I don't offer that." I can imagine that this man walked away knowing that he was unwilling to pay the price for discipleship. Then Jesus turned to another and said, "Follow Me." But the man responded, "Lord, first let me go and bury my father." And Jesus gave a shocking response. He said, "Let the dead bury their own dead, but you go and proclaim the kingdom of God." (Luke 9:60 NIV) You may wonder, "What is wrong with one taking care of some family business before following Jesus?" You may even be tempted to accuse Jesus of being insensitive and lacking sympathy. But I'll tell you one thing; If being a disciple of Jesus has not cost you anything, I'd strongly urge you to evaluate whether or not you are on the right path, because walking in the path of God will always come at a cost.

I like to say, don't subject the wisdom of God to human reasoning. God doesn't think like a man and He will never succumb to the thinking patterns of men. The God that said "follow Me" already considered that you had some family business to attend to; yet, His call required your immediate obedience. In other words, there is nothing that should come between you and God's instructions to you. I have seen so many miss out on and lose their God-assignments because of their family business. Saints, somethings can wait; your family business can wait, but the instructions of God are time-bound. Mary said to Jesus' disciples in John 2:5 (NKJV), "Whatever He says to you, do it!" In other words, don't consider the cost; do it quickly! If God says, forgive, then do it quickly! If He asks you to minister to a colleague at work, do it quickly! Whatever He tells you to do, do it quickly, before doubt comes in. The fellow who had the excuse of wanting to bury his father missed out on an opportunity to have his father raised back to life by placing his father's burial as a condition for his obedience. Martha made the same mistake when Jesus came to visit her and her siblings. She was so busy taking care of the family business, that she shoved off listening to what Jesus had to say. She must have forgotten that Jesus fed five thousand men, not counting women and children from a young lad's lunch.

Saints, the Lord is calling for radical obedience. When Peter asked Jesus what the gain was for those who followed Him recklessly or who were radical with their obedience, Jesus said, "... I assure you that everyone who has given up house or wife or brothers or parents or children, for the sake of the Kingdom of God, will be repaid many times over in this life, and will have eternal life in the world to come." (Luke 18:28-30 (NLT)) In other words, the cost of your obedience pales in comparison to what you'd get in return. I like to say that your obedience to God will always bring you more than you bargained for. Serving God will come at a cost, but the gain it brings will more than double whatever you lost. So, don't hold back. The next time you go to church, ask how you can make a difference.

Faith-Filled Confession:
Father, I thank You for giving me an excellent spirit with which I serve You and those around me. I will serve Your people wholeheartedly and without contempt. Thank You for Your ability that is at work in me, enabling me both to desire and to work out Your good purpose, in Jesus' name, Amen

SERVE REGARDLESS

"But love your enemies, do good to them, and lend to them, expecting nothing in return. Then your reward will be great, and you will be sons of the Most High; for He is kind to the ungrateful and wicked." (Luke 6:35 BSB)

Everywhere you turn, you can find countless reasons for not serving as you would Christ. The world has many reasons why you shouldn't serve as God expects. From the imperfection of a spouse, children who are acting up, co-workers who are difficult to deal with, to strangers who have a bad attitude. All these and more can present as justifiable reasons for not serving as God expects. God saw all of these things and still instructed you to serve people like you would Christ. To God, these imperfections were His motivation for ministering to the world by sending Jesus. So, if you are looking for a reason not to serve, you don't have to look anymore because there will always be one in front of you. The question, however, is this: "How will you handle these excuses for not serving that present themselves daily?"

Jeremiah 20:7-9 (NIV) paints a picture of a prophet of God who had had enough with serving people; primarily because of the way he was treated by those he was called to serve. Many times, we expect things to go smoothly because we have been sent by God; yet, the opposite is usually the case. Those that we have been anointed to serve are not always angels, spirit-filled, loving, or kind. Many times, we are sent to those who are anti-Christ and with the worst imaginable behavior. Jeremiah got to the point where he felt like he had had enough. He said to God, "You deceived me, Lord, and I was deceived; You overpowered me and prevailed. I am ridiculed all day long; everyone mocks me. Whenever I speak, I cry out proclaiming violence and destruction. So, the Word of the Lord has brought me insult and reproach all day long. But if I say, 'I will not mention His word or speak any more in His name, 'His word is in my heart like a fire, a fire shut up in my bones. I am weary of holding it in; indeed, I cannot."

Thank God that the Word of God burned in Jeremiah. Even with that, he still gave in to the pressure of discouragement. But the

31

Word in him was too strong for the spirit of discouragement. Just imagine if the Word of God had not been in him at all. He could have stopped because the people were mean and nasty and not deserving of his time.

Saints, I wish I could tell you that there was a justifiable reason for not doing as God has commanded you to do. But there is none. That your spouse, co-worker, church member, neighbor, or relative is obnoxious will not hold as a valid reason for failing to serve them as you would Christ. Jesus said, "But to those of you who will listen, I say: Love your enemies, do good to those who hate you, bless those who curse you, pray for those who mistreat you. If someone strikes you on one cheek, turn to him the other also. And if someone takes your cloak, do not withhold your tunic as well. Give to everyone who asks you, and if anyone takes what is yours, do not demand it back. Do to others as you would have them do to you. If you love those who love you, what credit is that to you? Even sinners love those who love them. If you do good to those who do good to you, what credit is that to you? Even sinners do the same. And if you lend to those from whom you expect repayment, what credit is that to you? Even sinners lend to sinners, expecting to be repaid in full. But love your enemies, do good to them, and lend to them, expecting nothing in return. Then your reward will be great, and you will be sons of the Most High; for He is kind to the ungrateful and wicked. Be merciful, just as your Father is merciful." (Luke 6:27-36 NIV)

Serve and don't stop serving. Heaven is counting on you.

Faith-Filled Confession:
The Word of God is my inspiration for all that I do. Christ is my motivation for service. I will seek to serve at every opportunity as I would Christ and will allow His love to flow through me to those around me.

faith

When you understand faith, the quality of your life
will be enhanced

Communion

FAITH IS NOT AN OPTION

It is written: 'I believed; therefore, I have spoken.' Since we have that same spirit of faith, we also believe and therefore speak." (2 Corinthians 4:13 NIV)

Faith is not an option to a child of God. It may seem to be for so many; yet, the Father's intent was never for any of us to have faith as an option. Repeatedly, the Bible declares that "the just shall live by faith." (Hebrews 10:38, Romans 1:17, Galatians 3:11 and Habakkuk 2:4) Meaning, there is no living outside of faith. Faith is your element, just as water is to fish. 1 Thess 2:12 (KJV) declares, "... who calls you into His kingdom and glory." God has called you into His kingdom and glory that operates by faith. To be called means to be born again. When you are born again, you are born into the kingdom of faith. Everything is faith-based. Papa God is a faith God; the language of the kingdom is called faith.

Think about the frustration that sometimes exists between a mother and her infant. The baby is communicating in perfect language and gets upset when his mother doesn't understand what he is saying. On the other hand, the mother is upset that she is doing everything to comfort the baby, yet the baby would not stop crying. The problem in this scenario is that the mother and child speak two different languages. If this child grows up and continues to communicate in the same manner, we would consider it to be a developmental challenge. A challenge that could hinder the quality of life lived. It is the same way with Papa God and you. The only difference is that God does not get upset at you. This is why when our children learn to speak our language; our hearts are filled with joy because now, we can communicate better! The same goes for the Father. When you begin to speak the language of faith, which is the language of the Father, heaven rejoices and joy explodes in the Father's heart.

Here is what happened when you got born again, Romans 12:3 (KJV) says that "God hath dealt to every man the measure of faith," meaning that there is no child of God that has a faith problem. The faith seed inside you right now is commensurate to what the Father used in the creation of the world in Genesis. In fact, it's the same level of faith according to 2 Corinthians 4:13.

How did God create the heavens and the earth with that level of faith and I can't get my bills paid? The answer lies in that same verse. It says, "I believed; therefore, I have spoken...." (2 Corinthians 4:13 NIV) Meaning, whatever He saw in His spirit, He spoke it into being. Then He said, since we have the same spirit of faith, we ought to believe and therefore speak it forth.

What do I believe? Believe the Word! Believe the word concerning your family, health, finance, business etc. Find out what the Word says. Do not take man's word for it. Get in the Word and let the Word get into you and when you have it on the inside of you, speak it forth! Hebrews 13:5-6 (NASB) shows us how it works, "... for He Himself has said, "I WILL NEVER DESERT YOU, NOR WILL I EVER FORSAKE YOU," so that we boldly say, "THE LORD IS MY HELPER, I WILL NOT BE AFRAID. WHAT WILL MAN DO TO ME? (NASB)

As a child of God, you have inside of you, God's creative ability and power. You have the ability to create and recreate your world. In John 10:10 (NLT), Jesus said, "My purpose is to give them a rich and satisfying life." And you have this life right now, so go ahead and live it to the maximum by faith. Praise God! Remember, to live by faith is to live in accordance with every Word that proceeds out of the mouth of Papa God. Believe the Word! Speak the Word! Live the Word! Let the Word of God govern your actions and inactions.

Faith-Filled Confession:
Father, in Isaiah 33:24, You said that "no resident [of Zion] will say, "I am sick"; The people who dwell there will be forgiven their iniquity." Therefore, I boldly declare that I walk in divine health. I declare that sin has no dominion over me. I walk in righteousness because I am the righteousness of God in Christ Jesus.

BELIEVE THE WORD WITH YOUR LIFE

"If you remain in Me and My words remain in you, ask whatever you wish, and it will be done for you." (John 15:7 NIV)

For so long, I wondered why many who were born again and filled with the Spirit, lived without the glow of God's presence. Then, the Lord said to me, "It is because they haven't believed in the glory beyond salvation." Their faith has failed to move past being saved from hell. Yet, the irony is that Jesus not only saved us from hell. His death also made it possible for us to have eternal life, and to have eternal life is to be born of God. 1 Peter 1:23 (KJV) says, "Being born again, not of corruptible seed, but of incorruptible, by the Word of God, which liveth and abideth forever." So, if you are born again, you are not just a believer in God. You are more than a believer! You are an HEIR of JEHOVAH! Romans 8:17 says that we are JOINT-HEIRS with Christ, and so, everything that belongs to Jesus Christ belongs to us in the same full measure. Jesus does not have it more and we do not have it less. Hallelujah!

Absolute peace, victory, and plenty are yours as an heir. Believe this! Jesus said that in Him you would have peace and you are in HIM; not in the world (John 16:33). In John 10:10 (NLT), Jesus said, "The thief's purpose is to steal and kill and destroy. My purpose is to give them a rich and satisfying life." And every child of God has this rich and satisfying life right now; we received this life at salvation. So our experiences or the experiences of others can neither validate nor disprove the Word of God. The Word of God is Truth regardless, and Jesus has done all that He needed to do for us to enjoy our best life now. It is now our turn to live out that life to the praise of Jesus Christ.

Your position as a child of God is to believe what God has done; not as one who is religious, but as a child. Because children believe without questioning and they share it with others without reservation, whether true or false. The good news, however, is that every Word of God is true and settled. He says what He means and means what He says. Hebrews 6:17-18 (BSB) says, "So when God wanted to make the unchanging nature of His purpose very clear to the heirs of the promise, He guaranteed it with an oath. Thus by two unchangeable things in which God can't lie..."

So in the light of the unchanging nature of the Word, look again at what Jesus said in John 15:7 and I want you to believe this with your life because it will put you over in every situation. Jesus said, "If you remain in Me and My words remain in you, ask whatever you wish, and it will be done for you. (BSB)" The interesting thing about these words is the power that it puts in your hands. Jesus said ask whatever you wish, not what God desires but what you desire. And when you ask, Jesus said that it would be done. The word that is translated "done" in this verse is the Greek word *ginomai*; which means to come into being. In other words, God doesn't have to do anything for this to happen. Jesus is simply saying that if you maintain fellowship with Him, you have access to everything you desire. The key, however, is fellowship and intimacy. When we ask from a place of intimacy, there is a creative power that is unleashed to bring things into being, even as it was with the Father in Genesis.

So, remember that you have all that you require to live a life of absolute peace, victory and plenty and your job is to be about living this glorious life.

Faith-Filled Confession:
The grace, favor, and spiritual blessing of the Lord Jesus Christ; the love of God; and the presence and fellowship, communion, sharing together, and participation in the Holy Spirit is with me today and forever. Amen.

FACT VS FAITH

But without faith it is impossible to please Him: for he that cometh to God must believe that He is, and that He is a rewarder of them that diligently seek Him. (Hebrews 11:6 KJV)

Faith for the Christian is non-negotiable. It is practically impossible for you to live the God-life without faith because the kingdom that you belong to functions primarily by faith. As water is to the fish, so is faith to the child of God. The scripture says that "the just shall live by faith" and the Greek word that translates "live" means lifestyle. This means that faith is not a tool that we use when things aren't going our way or when we try to get God to do something. Rather, faith is everything as a child of God. It is what defines who we are, what we have and what we can do in Christ Jesus.

Faith is living in the word of God. It is a lifestyle that accentuates the reality of Christ's triumphant conquest over hell, darkness, and death. It's a lifestyle that amplifies and enforces the testimony of Jesus over the government of hell and the senses, and if there is one thing the devil is after in these last days, it is the lifestyle of faith. To some, faith is wishful thinking and to others, faith is wishful speaking. However, to us, it is our life! It is not wishful thinking to live every day in absolute victory over hell, darkness, and death. Rather, it is absolute reality! We know who we are. Praise God!

You may have heard statements like these: "Let's get real with the fact, you have the flu, just say you have the flu." Or "You are broke, own up to it." But you see, as God's reproduction, we function by a different reality. We function by another knowledge that is not influenced by material elements. To us, faith does not deny the fact. What faith does is it denies the ability of that fact to alter our glorious experiences. We talk and act differently because of what we know to be true. My victory is truth. Therefore, I proclaim that I live in absolute victory every day. I refuse to endorse by my action or words any form of defeat. Praise God! You may not realize this, but God is not as concerned about the challenges you face as

39

He is about what you say and how you respond to the challenges that come your way. If as Christians, we believe that God's word is final authority, then we should be able to consider Joel 3: 10 (KJV) where the word of God says, "let the weak say, I am strong." Notice, this scripture did not deny that some were weak, yet it did not dwell on the weakness. God does not want the weakness empowered. He is concerned about your confessions. Notice, the Bible did not say let the weak face the fact that they are weak, rather, it says, let the weak say, "I am strong."

When you walk in faith, you are walking in obedience knowing that God honors His word. You are living a lifestyle that accentuates the reality of Christ's triumphant conquest over hell, darkness, and death. It is a lifestyle that amplifies and enforces the testimony of Jesus over the government of hell and the senses. Decide to lose sight of the obvious (what you can see, feel, hear, smell and taste) and focus on the REALITY (God's word). Live out loud your faith life. Praise God!

Faith-Filled Confession:
I live a life of faith, a lifestyle that amplifies and enforces the testimony of Jesus over the government of hell and the senses. I refuse to lose sight of the glory of God's word concerning my health and finances. I am healed and I prosper. In the name of the Lord Jesus.

FAITH IS ALWAYS NOW

"NOW FAITH is the assurance (the confirmation, the title deed) of the things [we] hope for, being the proof of things [we] do not see and the conviction of their reality [faith perceiving as real fact what is not revealed to the senses]." (Hebrews 11:1 AMP)

There is something about being born again that we must be accustomed to if we are ever going to walk in the greater glory. There are so many of God's people asking this question: "Why does the Bible say one thing and my life say something else?" The lingering effect of this question has led so many in the path of frustration and unbelief. For some, it has even caused them to question their salvation and the integrity of the Word of God. It ought not to be so. No Christian should ever question the validity of Christ's victory on the cross.

If as a young Christian, you were not taught properly on the faith lifestyle; chances are that you will ask the same question. As a Christian, you must understand that faith is not a tool; it is a lifestyle - your lifestyle. Hallelujah!

So why is there a disconnection? Why does the reality of the Word of God conflict with the experience of the individual that is born again? The answer is Faith. If a Christian will receive the Word of God as final authority regardless of any external factor and act accordingly, it will be impossible to experience less than God has made available. Whatever experience a person has or the reality they walk in, it is a direct result of what their faith is anchored on. If you act on the Word, you will walk in the glory of the Word and if you act on the senses, you will also get whatever the senses produce.

For example, there are many Christians around the world who are praying to be saved and hoping that they will receive eternal life when they get to heaven. It does not matter how honest they sound and look or how many hours they invest in such prayers; it is an exercise in futility and simply put, it is ignorance gone on a rampage. It is not faith and cannot produce faith. The reason is that it's not based on the Word of God. Faith says I have eternal life now. It is not something that I am going to have, I have it right now. In John 3:15 (ESV) the scripture declares "that whoever believes in Him should not perish but have eternal life." Did you notice, it does not say the believer is going to have eternal life; rather it says the believer is a possessor of eternal life. In other words, faith is affirming that what God says you are, you are now; what God says you have, you have now, and what God says you can do, you possess the ability to do so now irrespective of your senses or prevailing circumstance.

When you understand faith, the quality of your life will be enhanced. Let me show you another example, 1 John 4:4 AMP says "Little children, you are of God [you belong to Him] and have [already] defeated and overcome them [the agents of the antichrist], because He Who lives in you is greater (mightier) than he who is in the world." If you observe the tenses closely, you would notice that you have already defeated and overcome Satan and his cohort. Therefore, faith does not hope, wish or pray to overcome the devil. Rather, faith takes the position of a VICTOR over Satan, hell, and death. Praise God!

Faith-Filled Confession:
I walk in divine health every day. Sickness has no dominion over my body. In the name of the Lord Jesus Christ. I will say of the Lord that He is my refuge and fortress. My present help in times of need. Praise God!

FAITH AND THE WORD

> *"And there sat a certain man at Lystra, impotent in his feet, being a cripple from his mother's womb, who never had walked: The same heard Paul speak: who steadfastly beholding him, and perceiving that he had faith to be healed, said with a loud voice, stand upright on thy feet. And he leaped and walked." (Acts 14:8-10 KJV)*

Notice, the man had faith to be healed. His faith got turned on, hearing the Word of God from the lips of the Apostle. It means that the words that came out of the mouth of the Apostle were faith-filled words. Those words were filled with faith and power to effect change. Remember that this man was described as one who was impotent in his feet and crippled from his mother's womb and had never walked. If this is not a picture of a hopeless situation, I don't know what you would call it. Amazingly, his condition did not keep him from the house of God - the place where the Word of God was taught with power. Praise God!

He could have said, "You know I am crippled; I can't go." He could have come up with one excuse or another and it would have been understood. Nonetheless, he chose to position himself at a place for a miracle. Do you know how many people have missed the time of God's visitation? Do you know how the little things of this world have cost so many their miracles because they were not conscious of God's hour of visitation? This is why you must not treat the place where God's varieties are unveiled continuously as a commonplace. Think about it, even though he was impotent in his feet, he gave attention to the word of God. This is the part that should get you shouting! The man gave attention to the Word of God! Hallelujah!!

Listen! No one in the history of mankind gave attention to the Word of God that remained ordinary. No one! Everyone that gave attention to the Word of God became the Word of God in manifestation.

There is something extraordinary you can't afford to miss in this testimony. It is that the man's faith came alive listening to the Apostle.

43

However, that was not all, because his faith coming alive did not change his situation, until the word was given – the RHEMA WORD. Why was this so important? It was so important because faith has to respond to the Word. Not just any word, but a Rhema Word.

There have been times as I taught the Word that I perceived faith rising in those I was sharing the word with even as this man's faith was stirred. And while I was still sharing, a Rhema Word came out of my mouth directed at someone – a "NOW" word came forth and there was no response and I just kept sharing. If this man hadn't responded to the Rhema Word, he would have died in the same condition in which he was born – impotent, cripple and lame.

Rhema is God's now-word, directed specifically to you, for your situation. It may be from the lips of the man of God or a prompting of the Holy Spirit on the inside of you. To this man, the Rhema Word was: "Stand upright on thy feet." I don't know what your situation is right now. However, one thing I can tell you is that in every situation, there is a Rhema Word.

So, the next time your faith gets turned on, it may be in church or in your personal fellowship or maybe as you study and meditate on the Word. Look out for your Rhema Word with your spirit. It is that word that dissolves fear and awakens you to the realities of Christ. When you have it, don't stop talking about it. Rejoice, dance and shout, because you have a miracle! Praise God!

Faith-Filled Confession:
My life is beautiful and colored with love and prosperity by the Holy Ghost. Therefore, I refuse to walk in bitterness. I refuse to walk in offense. I refuse to walk in confusion. In the name of Lord Jesus Christ. I am anointed! I am anointed! I am anointed! Glory to God!

THE SIMPLICITY OF FAITH

"His mother said to the servants, "Whatever He says to you, do it." (John 2:5, NKJV)

This is one of the most remarkable statements made in the Bible on the subject of faith. This is how simple faith is but religion has made it so complicated that many of God's people have little or no understanding on the subject of faith. Faith by the way is more than a subject in the scriptures. It is the ecosystem of the Christian life. In Hebrews 10:38, the Bible says, "but my righteous one shall live by faith, and if he shrinks back, my soul has no pleasure in him." (NASB) The Greek word that translates to "live" is *zaō*. It means to experience God's gift of life. In other words, without faith, you cannot experience, demonstrate or manifest the God-life. To experience the God-life means that your life has become an exhibition of the effect of Christ's abiding victory over hell and death. It is living in the dominion of the Spirit. Think about everything that Jesus died to make available to you; prosperity, peace, victory, health, and the list goes on. To have all of these characterize your everyday life is what it means to experience, demonstrate and manifest the divine life. Praise God!

Mary had an understanding of the operation of the Spirit. She had previously encountered the spirit of faith. When Gabriel appeared and gave her the Word concerning the birth of Jesus, her initial response was "How can this be, since I do not know a man?" Then the angel explained the message and concluded with "For with God nothing will be impossible." (Luke 1:37, Webster's Bible Translation) In other words, the angel said to her, "No word from God is void of power." (ERV) I believe by this time her faith was already stirred. She responded with a confession in the affirmative. She said, "Let it be done to me according to your Word." Meaning that she used her confession to mix her faith with the Word and that was how a miracle was brought forth. She simply acted on the Word with her confession, because that particular message from God required a response.

45

Not only was Mary acquainted with the spirit of faith and living by faith; she also knew the anointing that was on Jesus. She likely had seen that power in demonstration privately. Why else would she say to Jesus, "They have no wine"? (John 2:3, NKJV) Remember that Jesus was a guest, not the host. That question should have been directed to the host. The fact that Mary told Him that they ran out of wine was an indication that she was expecting a miracle. Even after Jesus responded with, "Woman what does your concern have to do with me? My hour has not yet come." (NKJV) She anticipated that Jesus would instruct the disciples on what to do. So, she proceeded to instruct them on how to respond to His instructions. She said, "Whatever He says to you, do it." (John 2:5, NKJV) In other words, no matter how ridiculous and stupid He may sound, JUST DO IT! Because no word that proceeds from Him is void of power.

This is how simple faith is. There are no add-ons. JUST DO THE WORD, without which you cannot please God. In Hebrews 11:6, the Bible declares, "Now without faith, it is impossible to please God...." (ISV) Why so? It is because the proof that you love God is that you do His Word. Jesus said, "If you love me, you will keep my commandments." (ESV) In other words, if you love me, live by faith. And to live by faith is to live the divine life. For this reason, you must get addicted to the Word of God. Study the Bible for yourself and be everything that the Word says concerning you in Christ Jesus.

Faith-Filled Confession:
Father in the name of the Lord Jesus, I give you praise for the in-working power of the Spirit that has made me an exhibition of the miraculous and a vessel of bliss. Thank You for giving me a life of excellence and power, health and prosperity, victory and dominion, favor and success. Thank you, Father, that Jesus is Lord! Hallelujah!

DO EVERYTHING ACCORDING TO THE WORD

"With all this going for us, my dear, dear friends, stand your ground. And don't hold back. Throw yourselves into the work of the Master, confident that nothing you do for him is a waste of time or effort." (1 Corinthians 15:58 MSG)

Anything that is not founded on the Word of God

will ultimately fail, and it doesn't matter that it is named after Jesus. The key to success and victory is in listening to the Word and in doing as the Word instructs. Jesus said, "Why do you call Me 'Lord, Lord,' and not do what I tell you?" (Luke 6:46) In other words, Jesus was saying, "Why do you try to make Me a rubber stamp to your agenda?" Here's an example of how people do this. A drug dealer paying tithe on his drug earnings and expecting for his business to be blessed by God is trying to make God a stamp to His agenda and such an individual can only be described as a joker. Paying tithes and attending church services will not change the destiny of such business or the destiny of such an individual. Jesus went on to say in Luke 6:47-49, "Everyone who comes to Me and hears My Words and does them, I will show you what he is like: he is like a man building a house, who dug deep and laid the foundation on the rock. And when a flood arose, the stream broke against that house and could not shake it, because it had been well built. But the one who hears and does not do them is like a man who built a house on the ground without a foundation. When the stream broke against it, immediately it fell, and the ruin of that house was great." This lets us know that the issue is not with the size of the opposition; rather, it is with the foundation upon which we build.

God is not as concerned as most people think He is, about the size of your problem. He knows that the Word in you will always prevail. If you want to see victory manifested as the Word says, then your priority must be on the Word. Just saying "that is good stuff" in response to a message will not move a needle. That you serve and give, though necessary, will also not suffice. Your service and giving ought to stem from your obedience to the Word.

Doing the Word must take center stage in your life because God does nothing without the Word and He will not ignore the Word because of your situation. The scripture says, "He can't deny Himself" (2 Timothy 2:13) because He is one with His Word (John 1:1). From the creation of the heavens and the earth to Jesus raising the dead, it was all the result of the Word.

I heard about a fellow who came to his Pastor seeking financial assistance. He lamented about how serious and dire his situation was and was hoping for the pastor to issue him a check. Being sympathetic to his plight and moved by the Spirit, the pastor gave him some books to read and messages to listen to. As you would expect, with a surprised look, the brother asked, "Is that all?" Now, I know some people may be disappointed with this pastor, on the ground that he could have helped him out financially and later offered the books and messages. However, that is a very wrong idea! The Pastor knew something that you don't know. Because the problem with that fellow was not money; he lacked foundation in the Word concerning finances and no amount of money could solve his financial problem until he got his foundation right and the right foundation is the foundation of the Word.

I encourage you to do everything according to the Word. Your success and wellbeing are rooted in it. Audit your life and ensure that the Word is the foundation for all things. See to it that the Word is the final authority in all your affairs. Learn to rest and flourish in the Word, for in the Word is the fountain of success, healing, increase, prosperity, peace, joy and all that is good.

Faith-Filled Confession:
Thank You, Lord, for Your grace and faithfulness. I thank You for Your ability that is at work in me. Thank You for Your Word which is my sure guide. I thank You that I am not in the dark. You have made me the light and You have caused me to dwell in the light, where I am out of range to every form of evil. Thank You for good health of mind and body, peace, joy, miracles, increase and testimonies.

PUT THE WORD BEFORE YOU, IT WILL NEVER FAIL YOU

"Though your beginning was insignificant, yet your end will increase greatly." (Job 8:7)

In Mark 11:14, Jesus said to the fig tree, "No man eat fruit of thee hereafter forever..." And it appeared at the moment that the words of Jesus had no consequence on the tree because nothing happened. Some would have expected that as soon as Jesus gave the Word that some mysterious fire would have come down from Heaven to devour the tree. But that did not happen. Jesus gave the Word and walked away. He knew that His Word would not return to Him void. Hence, His focus was no longer on the tree, but on the anointing that the Word carried. Things may not look like they will turn out to be what God has said at the moment, but if you would keep your attention on the anointing and not be moved by how uncertain things may feel or look right now, sooner or later you will see the outpouring manifestation of what the Lord has said. In Luke 17:11-14 the Bible said that ten stood afar off and said, "Jesus, Master, have mercy on us!" When Jesus saw them "...He said to them, "Go, show yourselves to the priests." The lepers could have focused on their disease-ravaged body, but instead, they turned their attention to the Word. And it was that as they went, they were cleansed. What a miracle!

Remember, Habakkuk 2:3 says, "For the revelation awaits an appointed time; it speaks of the end and will not prove false. Though it lingers, wait for it; it will certainly come and will not delay." Maybe what you have heard from the Lord is beyond your imagination. And at the moment, everything in you is screaming, "how in the world, am I going to get this done?" Hear what the Spirit is saying to you right now: "God will make this happen, for He who calls you is faithful." (1b Thessalonians 5:24) And if I were you, I would bind these words around my neck. Because in the Word is the anointing that will bring about all that you require (people, finances, contact etc.). As the Lord said concerning Zerubbabel, He is saying to you today, "Do not despise these small beginnings, for the Lord rejoices to see the work begin..." This may be your silent season, but you must rejoice at the anointing. You must focus on what is working right now and not on the imperfections. Because many have missed out on God because they took their eyes away from the anointing and laid it on the temporal imperfections. Guard your heart against discouragement and thoughts of frustration. Rejoice!

Let your focus be on the anointing of the Word, don't allow the progress of others ruin your destiny in God. They are on their God calendar and you are on your God calendar, so enjoy the season that you are in! Hebrews 6:11-12 says "We want each of you to show the same diligence to the very end, so that your hope may be fully assured. Then you will not become spiritually dull and indifferent. Instead, you will follow the example of those who are going to inherit God's promises because of their faith and endurance." In other words, be patient.

Finally, "Though your beginning was insignificant, yet your end will increase greatly." (Job 8:7) Stay focused on the Word, because the anointing of the Word is working wonders on your behalf.

Faith-Filled Confession:
My eyes are fixed on Jesus, the author and the finisher of my faith. I am not moved by the transient circumstances of life. No matter the season, my foundation is on the Word of God. For the path of the righteous is like the morning sun, shining ever brighter till the full light of day. It only gets better for me. He has caused all things to work together for my good. I rejoice in Jesus. Hallelujah!

JUST DO THE WORD

"So if you are presenting a sacrifice at the altar in the Temple and you suddenly remember that someone has something against you, leave your sacrifice there at the altar. Go and be reconciled to that person. Then come and offer your sacrifice to God." (Matthew 5:23-24 NLT)

As a young Christian, I was always concerned whenever I saw a Christian in an unending circle of conflicts. And as I got to understand the Scriptures better, I realized that when one has the Holy Spirit, such should not be their story. Any Christian who finds themselves in such a place, I can tell you in no uncertain terms, has not been listening to the Holy Spirit. Jesus sent the Holy Spirit to be our guide, and the Holy Spirit does not lead us in circles, but forward and upward; with Him, we make progress.

Several years ago, a pastor, known to me, was involved in an accident that almost took his life and the life of his wife. When the report of the accident came to me, I said to those around me, "There's no way that Satan could have successfully stuck him if he had listened to the Holy Spirit." I said that mainly because of the number of people that God had put under his spiritual care. A few weeks later, he said, "I almost killed my wife because I didn't listen to God." Had this pastor passed away, it would have been a huge loss to the church and would not have brought honor to God because his assignment here was not yet complete.

Psalm 23:3 says, "He renews my strength. He guides me along right paths, bringing honor to His name." The Holy Spirit renews our strength and guides us in such a way that brings honor to God. You would agree that suffering to make ends meet or being oppressed by sickness does not bring God any honor. We have the Holy Spirit to lead us in the path of light, not darkness. So if you ever find yourself in the way of darkness, you have the Holy Spirit to deliver you out of it. Obedience to the leading of the Holy Spirit is the way to enjoy health and increase every day. I'll say it again; suffering is unnecessary if you are born again and filled with the Holy Spirit. If you would listen to Him and follow His guidance, your life will be nothing short of the glory of the Word.

In Matthew 5:23-24, Jesus gave an instruction that, when followed, sets you up for glory. He said, "...if you are presenting a sacrifice at the altar in the Temple and you suddenly remember that someone has something against you, leave your sacrifice there at the altar. Go and be reconciled to that person. Then come and offer your sacrifice to God." In other words, God will not receive anything from you as long as you have bitterness in your heart. And if God will not receive anything from you, it means that you cannot receive anything from Him. As simple as this instruction is, many Christians have ignored it; they walk around with bitterness in their hearts, hoping that their prayers will be answered. Yet, their answers lie in their obedience.

Child of God, there's no need to suffer. Just do the Word!

God bless you!

Faith-Filled Confession:
My heart is open to the ministry of the Holy Spirit today. I give myself to correction and instruction in righteousness. Spirit of God, I am yours to command today in Jesus' name. Amen.

forgiveness

Forgiveness is a gift and not something
that should be earned

Communion

OVERLOOK AN OFFENSE

"Good sense makes one slow to anger, and it is his glory to overlook an offense." (Proverbs 19:11, ESV)

It is important to know that God being present in itself, changes nothing. What changes the situation is when we act on what God has said. Case in point; Lazarus was dead and buried for four days and Jesus arrived at his grave, yet nothing happened. Jesus just being present at the grave of Lazarus did not bring Lazarus back to life until Jesus gave the word: "Lazarus, come forth!" (John 11:43, KJV) Many times, ever before we speak, God has already spoken about our particular circumstance, and our miracle lies in what we do with what He already said. And if there is one thing that hinders a child of God from hearing and acting on the anointing of the Holy Spirit, it is offense.

Offense is like an odorless gas. You don't see or smell it but it is there causing damage; sometimes irrevocable. Let me give you an example of how subtle offense can be. In Luke 10, the Bible records that Jesus visited the house of Mary and Martha. Upon getting there, He began to teach and Martha being the hospitable person that she was, went to prepare a meal for her guest. Mary, on the other hand, decided that she was going to listen to what He had to say. From this encounter, one may be tempted to blame Mary for not assisting her sister in ensuring that their guest was properly taken care of. Martha felt her sister was being inconsiderate. Eventually, she confronted Jesus saying, "Lord, do You not care that my sister has left me to serve alone? Tell her to help me!" At this point, Martha was to some extent, blaming Jesus for her sister's conduct. However, I love Jesus' reply. He said, "Martha, Martha," the Lord replied, "you are worried and upset about many things. But only one thing is necessary. Mary has chosen the good portion, and it will not be taken away from her." In other words, it wasn't just the fact that Mary didn't help her that got her upset, she was upset with Jesus, and maybe with Lazarus too.

Here was Martha getting into offense without her knowing it. She felt it was perfectly okay for her to question Jesus, but Jesus pointed out to her that the problem was not with Mary not assisting her. The problem was that she was offended by something that should not have offended her in the first place.

Offense is not just an emotion; it's an odorless gas that can abort one's destiny. Child of God, it's not worth your time and life to relive the same negative experience. Your destiny is way bigger than what someone said or how you were treated, because, at the end of the day, it accounts for nothing. And if you are having a hard time overcoming a negative emotion, ask the Lord for help. He is a present help; He is waiting to step in as soon as you invite Him. He wants to see you live fulfilled and happy.

Faith-Filled Confession:
The Word of God is my inspiration and source for counsel. I will diligently study the Word to gain wisdom and understanding of my purpose, walk, and destiny in God. And as I do, Christ is revealed to my spirit through His Word, in Jesus' name, Amen.

DON'T ENTERTAIN OFFENSE

"So then, let us aim for harmony in the church and try to build each other up." (Romans 14:19, NLT)

An environment that tolerates offense is a real danger because sooner than later, it becomes the reality of those in that environment. Here's what I mean: When one is comfortable with others operating under the spirit of offense, it will only be a matter of time before they too start functioning under the cloud of offense. An example of this is found in Numbers 12. Scripture declares that "Miriam and Aaron began to talk against Moses because of his Cushite wife, for he had married a Cushite." (NIV) In other words, Miriam was offended and got Aaron on board with her. She murmured out loud saying, "Has the Lord spoken only through Moses? Hasn't He also spoken through us?" And Aaron concurred. The problem here was not that she was telling a lie. It was the manner in which she said what she said. It was a slight to Moses and the Bible says, "the Lord heard it." (ESV)

I believe Aaron had the opportunity to prevent Miriam from walking into the impending danger of offense against the man of God, Moses. He could have counseled her to not take the bait of offense but he failed to recognize the demon of offense speaking through her. I would like to caution you by saying to you, whenever someone comes to you to air out their grievances about someone else, your first question before they go into any detail should be, "Have you brought this matter to the attention of this person?" Jesus said in Matthew 18:15, "If another believer sins against you, go privately and point out the offense. If the other person listens and confesses it, you have won that person back." (NLT) Jesus never said we should internalize the offense. The instruction was that we go to the person privately to address the issue. Anything short of that would be creating an atmosphere for offense to breed.

Child of God, do not entertain anything that contradicts the Word. You can no longer keep company with people who refuse to live by the standard of the Word. When people feel comfortable complaining about God's people around you, it's time to check your heart and motives. You can no longer hold on to relationships that dishonor the Word of God in your life. When you honor God's word above your feelings, you won't be afraid of the response of those who need to be corrected. And remember, any correction must be done in love because when you love someone the way God loves, you will not be afraid to correct their behavior.

Faith-Filled Confession:
I choose to obey God rather than men. I stand on the side of the Word of God regardless of the opposition. My life radiates the glory of God's Word. I shine as a light in the darkness. I live to please God and God alone and the benefits of doing the Word are evident in my life. In Jesus name

RESPOND WITH FORGIVENESS

"Anyone whom you forgive, I also forgive. Indeed, what I have forgiven, if I have forgiven anything, has been for your sake in the presence of Christ, so that we would not be outwitted by Satan; for we are not ignorant of his designs." *(2 Corinthians 2:10-11, ESV)*

There is a consciousness of personality that we must maintain as new creations. It is the consciousness of the Father's love that is poured forth in our hearts by the Holy Ghost. This consciousness that we are the reproduction of God's love is an absolute necessity. Until we grasp the immensity of this revelation, we will not know the true meaning of the divine life. Jesus said, "...love each other. Just as I have loved you, you should love each other." (John 13:34, NLT) Jesus wouldn't demand that we love with the same level and quality of love like He loved us if it was not possible. In other words, Jesus said, don't love like the rest of the world does, they don't know or have the nature of love. But you know and have the nature of love, you are born of Love. And this love nature is quick to forgive.

There is an adversary who would stop at nothing if allowed to devour all that belongs to us. Most illnesses are a result of unforgiveness. Satan knows this and so should you. There are so many of God's people who are weak and dying because they failed to understand the power of forgiveness. I am dealing with forgiveness that comes from the spirit and not from the head. When you forgive someone that did you harm, you actually benefit more than the one that wronged you. Your health, prosperity, transformation, growth, progress, success, and all that Grace has made available to you in Christ is dependent on it. Allow me to state it again; there is no reason why you should be living in misery and defeat, not after you have been born again! Learn to embrace the totality of who you are in Christ Jesus. Understand that when it comes to forgiveness, you must be proactive. You must be leaning towards those who are unkind to you with a tsunami of Christ's liquid love.

In 1 John 2:10 the Bible declares, "He that loves his brother abides in the light, and there is no occasion of stumbling in him." (KJV) The Greek word that translates "stumbling" is "skandalon". This is the same word from which we derive the word scandal. It is associated with failure, defeat and misery. To walk in forgiveness is a defensive mechanism for your spirit against failure, defeat and misery. Why do you think the enemy keeps playing those hurtful words and showing you those pictures of what was said and done to you? It is simply because he knows the power of unforgiveness. He knows that it will pollute your health and your vision and cause you to break the hedge so that he can legally come in and devour everything that belongs to you. Listen, walking in love that is proactive, coupled with forgiveness, are offensive weapons against sickness, confusion and depression.

When it comes to forgiveness, it is something you cannot afford to sleep over. You must forgive quickly because your life depends on it. You cannot wait for them to apologize. You must forgive quickly. Declare with your mouth, "I forgive (insert name) in the name of Jesus Christ. And I declare that I love you. In the name of Jesus." The Message translation puts it this way, "Be gentle with one another, sensitive. Forgive one another as quickly and thoroughly as God in Christ forgave you." (Ephesians 4:32, MSG) And in 2 Corinthians 2:10-11, the Apostle Paul stated, "Anyone whom you forgive, I also forgive... so that we would not be outwitted by Satan; for we are not ignorant of his designs." (ESV) Wake up and let go of any past offense. Rise up strong and tall. Rise above the bitterness of others and respond with forgiveness every time.

Faith-Filled Confession:
Father in the name of the Lord Jesus, I thank you for your grace and ability at work in me to forgive quickly and thoroughly. I refuse to think ill of those that have wronged me or anyone for that matter. I bless them with the favor of God. I celebrate their progress and prosperity. And I declare that no evil shall befall them. In the name of the Lord Jesus Christ.

BE STEADFAST IN FORGIVENESS

"Then Peter came to Jesus and asked, "Lord, how many times shall I forgive my brother or sister who sins against me? Up to seven times?" Jesus answered, "I tell you, not seven times, but seventy-seven times." (Matthew 18:21-22 NIV)

Forgiveness is a gift and not something that should be earned. If you wait for someone to own up to their wrong deed before you forgive them, it is no longer a gift, but a reward and such forgiveness does not carry the glow of Christ and has no eternal impact on the one that receives it. It was never God's design for forgiveness to be earned. It is a gift that is dependent on the character of the giver, not that of the receiver. Romans 5:8 says "But God demonstrates His own love for us in this: While we were still sinners, Christ died for us." (NIV) God's love which was poured out on us had nothing to do with us. Ever before we did wrong, He forgave us. The day that you confessed your sin was not the day that God forgave you. Your confession only connected you to the reality of His forgiveness. Ever before you said, "Lord, I am sorry," God already forgave you in Christ Jesus. The very day that the blood of Jesus was shed on the cross; your sins, past, and [peradventure] future were completely forgiven. Papa God forgave us from eternity to eternity and all we have to do is to receive His forgiveness as a gift.

Ephesians 4:32 says, "Be kind and compassionate to one another, forgiving each other, just as in Christ God forgave you." (NIV) If God gave you the gift of forgiveness, you should be willing to do the same for others; anything short of that is pride. Pride is waiting for someone to earn your forgiveness. As a new creation in Christ, you do not have the luxury of waiting around for someone to crawl to your feet and apologize before you forgive them. It's best that you forgive ever before you are wronged.

Child of God, you are too sweet to be bitter and too beautiful to walk in unforgiveness. There is nothing in this world that anyone can say or do to change the reality of Christ in your life. Leave bitterness and unforgiveness to those without the beauty of God in their spirits. Do you not realize that you are the epitome of beauty? Has it ever crossed your mind that you are a heavenly manifestation; the outshining of Christ, and the most beautiful being to have graced the earth? Wake up and let go of disappointments and betrayals of yesterday. Arise to your divinity and walk tall with love in your heart. Pour it out on those who misrepresented you and caused you harm in the past. Do not become a product of their bitterness or conform to their insecurities. Rise above it all and be the divine you that you really are. When they spill out anger and hatred towards you, respond with a tsunami of love. Praise God!

Peter asked, "Lord, how many times shall I forgive my brother or sister who sins against me?" (Matthew 18:21, NIV) In the mind of Peter, seven times was a stretch. Then the Lord said something that shocked Peter, He said, "I tell you, not seven times, but seventy-seven times." (Matthew 18:22, NIV) Jesus was saying in essence, "Do not keep a record. Forgive as many times as is necessary." Child of God, do not be slow to forgive and keep no record of wrongs done to you. Let your forgiveness be limitless.

Faith-Filled Confession:
I function with the consciousness that I have love, joy, peace, patience, kindness, goodness, faithfulness, gentleness and self-control. I live an excellent life, full of the demonstration of the Spirit and I forgive without hesitation.

hope

Even when there was no reason for hope,
Abraham kept hoping and believing
that he would become the father of many nations

YOU ARE A MIRACLE TO SOMEONE TODAY, DON'T QUIT!

"I'm sure now I'll see God's goodness in the exuberant earth. Stay with God! Take heart. Don't quit. I'll say it again: Stay with God." (Psalm 27:14 MSG)

Everything that God has done, and that God will ever do is centered on the person of Jesus. And because you are in Christ, as one divine creation with Him, Heaven's activities are centered on you as well. I know it may be hard for religion to swallow, but that is God's thought concerning you. He doesn't see you apart from Jesus, and His creation sees you in the same light — in the light of Christ. Colossians 1:16 says, "For in Him all things were created: things in heaven and on earth, visible and invisible, whether thrones or powers or rulers or authorities; all things have been created through Him and for Him." (NIV) Child of God, all things are for you.

You may not have known this, but demons are afraid of you because of the life of Christ in you. God said to Moses, "...See, I have made you like God to Pharaoh..." (Exodus 7:1, NIV) You are a force to be reckoned with in the earth. You are not an accident; you are not a victim of your past mistakes. You are a miracle worker; a blessing from Heaven. You are a God factor wherever you find yourself. Raise your heads high and do what you have been anointed to do. Make a difference in the lives of others. Give them a God-break in their situations. Praise God!

Set your mind right today. Everything that God will do today is for your promotion. Nothing that you encounter today is designed for your disadvantage. All that you will face has been given one purpose, and that is to bring God the glory through you. Believe that the anointing is upon you, causing you to win big. No matter what you see or feel, there's no going back. Don't desire to live a "normal" life when you have been anointed to live a supernatural life. Normal ended yesterday and yesterday ended last night. Yesterday may not have turned out the way you would have expected, but relax; today is a great opportunity to win with your spouse, church, community, and with the Holy Spirit. It's a new day! Stay with the Word! Take heart and don't quit because God has anointed you to be a miracle to someone today. Look out for a need and seek to add value to someone's life today.

Faith-Filled Confession:
My faith is unwavering. My trust is in God alone. I believe the Word of God with my whole being. And I know that He that has begun a good work in me will surely bring it to completion. I rejoice in Jesus! Amen

IT ONLY GETS BETTER

"But the path of the just [righteous] is like the light of dawn, that shines brighter and brighter until [it reaches its full strength and glory in] the perfect day." (Proverbs 4:18, AMP)

If you are born again, you have been born into a life of glory, and things can only get better for you. Your life only goes from strength to strength and from victory to victory. Your today is so much better than your yesterday, and your tomorrow will be so much better than your today. This should cause you to shout with joy! Just to know that each new day is greater and more glorious than the days past.

2 Corinthians 3:18 says, "And all of us, as with unveiled face, [because we] continued to behold [in the Word of God] as in a mirror the glory of the Lord, are constantly being transfigured into His very own image in ever-increasing increasing splendor and from one degree of glory to another; [for this comes] from the Lord [Who is] the Spirit." (AMPC) In other words, for your life to reflect the glory of God, you must go for the Word; you must feed on the Word like never before. The more you do so, the more your life is transformed into the glory of the Word and the more the glory is expressed in your daily experiences.

Proverbs 4:18 says, "But the path of the just (righteous) is like the light of dawn, that shines brighter and brighter until [it reaches its full strength and glory in] the perfect day." (AMP) Put yourself in this scripture and ask yourself this question: "Am I the righteous person here?" If you answered "yes", you then must confess it to be so, and speak God's Word over your life. By doing this, you are beholding (seeing) yourself in the mirror of the Word and the more you do this, the more you are transformed into the glory of the Word.

Begin today on a high note. See possibilities only. See with the eyes of God because His plans for you are so much bigger than you can fathom. Be unstoppable today because your life is from glory to glory.

Faith-Filled Confession:
I am special; I am not ordinary. The life of God is at work in me. I manifest the virtues and perfections of Christ. Today, I declare that my path is flooded with light; I do not stumble. I have the victory! In Jesus' name, Amen.

BRING FORTH THE SEED OF THE WORD

"...Mary said, "Behold, I am the servant of the Lord; let it be to me according to Your word." And the angel departed from her." (Luke 1:38, ESV)

God has deposited in you the seed of His Word concerning your life. He has deposited in you seeds of greatness; seeds of various ventures and groundbreaking ideas. It is now your responsibility to see that your experience lines up with what He has said concerning your life. It is also your responsibility to bring forth all that He has deposited in you. In Luke 1:31, an angel appeared to Mary with a Word from God saying, "You will conceive and give birth to a son, and you are to call Him Jesus." (NIV) Upon hearing these words, it was now Mary's choice to either believe or not believe the Word. She had to choose to either take hold of the Word or blow it off as impossible based on her circumstances at the time. But Mary chose to believe the impossible and receive the Word of God for her life. This is why we still talk about Mary today.

Child of God, there is a time for everything; a time to conceive and a time to bring forth. Just as a woman conceives seed, and in due time brings forth a child, so also, you are empowered to bring forth all that God has put in. Hebrews 11:11 says, "And by faith, even Sarah, who was past childbearing age, was enabled to bear children because she considered Him faithful who had made the promise." (NIV) The reason Sarah was able to conceive and bring forth a child even after she was past the age of childbearing was that she took a hold of the Word by faith. Child of God, it does not matter how long you have had that seed in you; the Lord has said that you will manifest all that He has put in you. It may look impossible in the natural but respond like Mary. For with God, nothing is impossible, and to him that believes, all things are possible.

I encourage you to believe the Word of God. Take a hold of God's Word and step out in faith knowing that the seed in you belongs to God, and He has made available to you all that is required to bring it forth. Listen to His directions and trust His guidance for He that has begun this good work in your life will surely bring it to completion.

Faith-Filled Confession:
My faith is unwavering; My trust is in God alone. I believe the Word of God with my whole being. And I know that He that has begun a good work in me will surely bring it to completion in Jesus' name, Amen!

DON'T HOLD BACK

"As the deer pants for the water brooks, so pants my soul for You, O God". (Psalm 42:1, NKJV)

There is no room for luke-warmness in your walk with God. You cannot serve God and serve the world at the same time. Jesus actually put it this way, "No man can serve two masters: for either he will hate the one, and love the other; or else he will hold to the one, and despise the other. Ye cannot serve God and mammon." (Matthew 6:24, KJV) Do not be deceived by those that suggest that you can be a Christian and live like the rest of the world at the same time. You have to choose; you've got a choice to make. Prophet Elijah was faced with people who tried to live a "two-faced" life, asked, "..."How long will you waver between two opinions? If the Lord is God, follow Him; but if Baal is God, follow him...." (1 Kings 18:21, NIV) Joshua, the man of God, said to the people of Israel, "But if serving the Lord seems undesirable to you, then choose for yourselves this day whom you will serve, whether the gods your ancestors served beyond the Euphrates, or the gods of the Amorites, in whose land you are living. But as for me and my household, we will serve the Lord." (Joshua 24:15, NIV) Joshua had his mind made up. He recognized that serving the gods of his ancestors was an option, but confidently declared that he and his household were going to serve the Almighty God. In doing this, he was forsaking all others. He made up his mind that his service to God was going to be with his whole heart.

The Patriarch, David's service to God was with passion and enthusiasm. He recognized God in everything. He recognized God as his source, strength, and sustainer. His service to God was with total abandonment. He served God with his whole heart. Even when he made a mistake, he was quick to cry out for forgiveness. While erring against God, he cried out, "Create in me a clean heart, O God; and renew a right spirit within me. Cast me not away from thy presence; and take not thy holy spirit from me." (Psalm 51:10-11, ESV) He knew that God's presence was life. In Psalm 42:1, He said, "As the deer pants for the water brooks, so pants my soul

71

for You, O God." (Psalm 42:1, NKJV) What a passion! Can the same be said of you?

Do not be deceived brethren; you are not missing anything out there in the world. In God *is* life. Let your service to God be with reckless abandon. With God, you can only win; you never lose. Jesus said, "If you don't go all the way with Me, through thick and thin, you don't deserve Me. If your first concern is to look after yourself, you'll never find yourself. But if you forget about yourself and look to Me, you'll find both yourself and Me." (Matthew 10:38-39 MSG) God desires your whole heart. Jesus said the most important commandment is to "love the Lord your God with all your heart and with all your soul and with all your mind and with all your strength." (Mark 12:30) In other words, love and serve God with your whole being; not half-heartedly or haphazardly.

Saints, God wants you to be on fire for Him. He wants you to go all the way! Even when others call you names. Don't hold back; let your service be with passion; be free to be all that He has called you to be.

Faith-Filled Confession:
As the deer pants for the water brooks, so pants my soul for You, O God. You, my God, are my source, strength, and sustainer. I choose to serve You with my whole being and with all that I have. Today, I declare that as for me and my household, we shall serve the Lord. Amen!

IT SHALL COME TO PASS

"Jesus looked at them and said, "With man it is impossible, but not with God. For all things are possible with God." (Mark 10:27, ESV)

I know it's hard sometimes to believe in something that is completely foreign to you. It can be hard to believe that you are what God says you are when all that you feel and see communicates something different. I get it! Mary the mother of Jesus felt the same way. She asked the angel, "How will this be since I am a virgin?" (Luke 1:34, NIV) In essence, she was saying, "I don't get it, but I am listening." And the angel replied, "The Holy Spirit will come upon you, and the power of the Most High will overshadow you. The Holy One to be born will be called the Son of God. Look, even Elizabeth your relative has conceived a son in her old age, and she who was called barren is in her sixth month. For nothing will be impossible with God." (Luke 1:35-37, Berean Study Bible) As Mary listened, the Word saturated her consciousness, and she said, "I am the Lord's servant. May everything you have said about me come true." (Luke 1:38, NLT) In other words, she was saying, "I may not feel or see how it's going to happen, but I trust God and because I trust God, I believe it will come to pass." She may have started out being unsure, but the Word birthed faith in her.

You may be in a precarious situation today, and you have everything around you telling you that there is no hope in sight. Allow me to encourage you today; don't allow the transient circumstances that you face to sway you away from your miracle. Things may not look right at the moment but that doesn't mean that they are that way. If God said you have something, believe it and conduct yourself in the light of what God has said. If God said you are going to accomplish something in your lifetime and it appears as though it's not going to happen, believe in God and not in your situation. Consider Mary. She had every reason to believe that as a virgin, it was impossible for her to have a child without the agency of a man. But the Word that she heard stirred faith in her, so much so that she said, "I am the Lord's servant. May everything you have said about me come true." (NLT) And according to the time of life, the Word which she received from God came to pass. I believe that's going to be your story as well. Yours is a story of a fulfilled life.

Each day, remind yourself of what God has said. Be consistent with your confession and be thankful that God's Word is settled. Also, do not neglect to walk in love and to be a helping hand to others who are in need. Let everything about you reflect that your trust is in God alone. As you do these things, the power of that situation will be weakened and the power of God in you will arise and eventually take over. Remember the Words of Jesus: "With man it is impossible, but not with God. For all things are possible with God." (Mark 10:27, ESV) And God is for you. So, cheer up! Everything will be alright.

Faith-Filled Confession:
Some may trust in chariots, some in horses, but my trust is in the name of the Lord my God. Those who know You, trust in You, for You, Lord, have never forsaken those who seek you. I trust in Your unfailing love and my soul rejoices in your salvation (Psalm 13:5; Psalm 9:10; Psalm 20:7).

PRESS ON

"For our light affliction, which is but for a moment, worketh for us a far more exceeding and eternal weight of glory."
(2 Corinthians 4:17, KJV)

You have outlasted every problem that you have had to face. No matter what it is that you are facing today, this too shall come to pass. Know that every storm that you face is designed to bring you a promotion. It may feel hard and unbearable sometimes but at the end of the day, it always works out right. So, press through the pressure! Don't crack underneath the weight on you. You can handle this! Child of God, you are not in this by yourself. It may appear as though you are alone in this, but believe me, you are not. Many others have felt this way, but here is the truth: 1 Corinthians 10:13 says, "No test or temptation that comes your way is beyond the course of what others have had to face. All you need to remember is that God will never let you down; He'll never let you be pushed past your limit; He'll always be there to help you come through it." (MSG)

David said in Psalm 139:1-6 TPT "Lord, you know everything there is to know about me. You perceive every movement of my heart and soul, and you understand my every thought before it even enters my mind. You are so intimately aware of me, Lord. You read my heart like an open book and you know all the words I'm about to speak before I even start a sentence! You know every step I will take before my journey even begins. You've gone into my future to prepare the way, and in kindness you follow behind me to spare me from the harm of my past. You have laid your hand on me! This is just too wonderful, deep, and incomprehensible! Your understanding of me brings me wonder and strength"

I have also come to know this about God; He moves on our behalf when we stop trying to figure it out without Him; when you start to trust in Him, you'll see Him do whatever He has said. You may have also heard The Lord say that "this too shall come to pass".

If you've heard Him say that, I stand with you today declaring that "this too shall pass". 2 Corinthians 4:17 says "For our light affliction, which is but for a moment, worketh for us a far more exceeding and eternal weight of glory." (KJV) In other words, every challenge that you face has already been deemed by God to be to your advantage. See this time as an opportunity for growth; see it as an opportunity to unleash your highest praise and worship. I know it hurts sometimes but I encourage you to worship Him even when it doesn't make sense.

Faith-Filled Confession:
I will bless the Lord at all times, and in every situation, I will bless His holy name. He has been my rock, sustainer, physician, provider, strength, help, protector, comforter, and counselor – He has been my EVERYTHING! I am a testimony of His grace, mercy, and love. He has been and remains MY GOD!

PRODUCTIVE DAY LIKE NOTHING EVER HAPPENED

"But go, tell his disciples and Peter, 'He is going ahead of you into Galilee. There you will see him, just as he told you.'" (Mark 16:7 NIV)

"I am not feeling my best today. I feel like going back to sleep and calling off work. From every indication, today is going to be rough and drossy. I feel sick to my stomach; I am restless and agitated because of all that happened yesterday. I wish I could delete all that happened yesterday from my mind, but I can't. And now I can't stop it from playing over and over in my head."

These are thoughts that come to you after you have had a not so great day. It could be as a result of a mistake you made at work that almost got you fired. Now, you have to return to work, and the thought of it is dreadful. Or maybe it is due to financial obligations from an accident in which you were at fault. These situations can lead to you feeling overwhelmed and confused if not properly handled.

Peter, who later became an apostle, had the same feelings when he denied Jesus three times. He left everything to follow Jesus, only to deny Him when it mattered the most. This was the same Peter, who was so confident in himself that he took Jesus aside to rebuke Him for saying that He would die and be raised from the dead after three days. It was the same Peter that walked on water. The same Peter was with Jesus on the mount of transfiguration, where he experienced something that only a few experienced. The same Peter was told by Jesus, "Flesh and blood has not revealed this to you but my Father in Heaven." Peter wasn't just a disciple; he was a senior disciple groomed by the Lord Himself to lead the church after His death. Peter was handpicked by Jesus to lead God's army (the church) after His ascension. Yet, the same Peter denied Jesus. Luke 22:61-62 (ESV) says, "And the Lord turned and looked at Peter. And Peter remembered the saying of the Lord, how He had said to him, "Before the rooster crows today, you will deny me three times." And he went out and wept bitterly."

So, before you write yourself off because of a mistake you have made, remember that Jesus did not write Peter off. And He has not written you off. Instead, the angel said to Mary in Mark 16:7 (NIV), "But go, tell his disciples and Peter, 'He is going ahead of you into Galilee. There you will see him, just as he told you.'" In other words, tell Peter that he is still part of God's plan. Whatever sin he committed did not disqualify him from God's plan.

God is saying, "whatever you have done has not disqualified you from my help. Your feeling of hopelessness, anxiety, depression, fear, and shame are not from Me. Yes, you were at fault. Yes, you sinned. But My help is still very much at your disposal like you didn't do anything wrong." So, collect forgiveness and put off that garment of sadness, depression, fear, and anxiety. Instead, say to yourself, "The Lord is my righteousness. He delights in my progress today." Now, get up and by the power of God advance and have a productive day like nothing ever happened.

Faith-Filled Confession:
Heavenly Father, I thank You that my life is full of beauty, glory, and excellence. I boldly confess that I am transformed, renewed, and ready to be used for that which pleases You today. Amen.

MAINTAIN THE INSPIRATION

"And said, O man greatly beloved, fear not: peace be unto thee, be strong, yea, be strong. And when he had spoken unto me, I was strengthened, and said, "Let my lord speak; for thou hast strengthened me." (Daniel 10:19, KJV)

Have you ever had the desire to do something, but

when it came time to do it, you seemed to lack the strength to follow through? Maybe you have said to yourself, "I am going to stay positive and walk in love no matter what is said or done to me," or "I am going to pray and study the Word every day" and it's been months now and you still have done nothing in the direction of your desire, and you wonder why? The answer is simple. It's the lack of inspiration or inner strength. For the church in Ephesus, Paul the Apostle anticipated and prayed for them knowing that they may lack the inspiration to do right by him and by the gospel. In his letter to them, he said, "I ask you, therefore, not to be discouraged because of my sufferings for you, which are your glory." (Ephesians 3:13, NIV) In other words, situations in our lives and in the lives of others can potentially drain out our inspiration and this is why Paul prayed for the church at Ephesus. He said, "I pray that out of His glorious riches He may strengthen you with power through His Spirit in your inner being, so that Christ may dwell in your hearts through faith. And I pray that you, being rooted and established in love, may have power, together with all the Lord's holy people, to grasp how wide and long and high and deep is the love of Christ, and to know this love that surpasses knowledge—that you may be filled to the measure of all the fullness of God." (Ephesians 3:16-19, NIV) Hallelujah!

In addition to prayer, the Word also can fan the embers of your inspirations. Daniel was in a situation where he required his faith in God to come alive. Afraid and weak, the Lord spoke to him. And Daniel said, "...And when He had spoken unto me, I was strengthened...." (Daniel 10:19, KJV) Daniel was strengthened by the Word of God to him. This tells us that the Word is a source of inspiration and strength to accomplishing all that God has called us to do. It also means that the Word can destroy doubt and fear. If you ever feel discouraged, get to the Word and pray in the spirit. When others tell you why it can't be done, get to the Word. When it looks like you are lacking the required support, get to the Word. When everything looks like you didn't hear from God, get to the Word. Whenever you hear or see things that communicate fear or discouragement, run to the Word. Better still, stay in the Word at all times regardless of the favorability of circumstances; just stay in the Word. Proverbs 6:21-23 says, "Bind them continually on your heart; tie them around your neck. When you walk about, they will guide you; when you sleep, they will watch over you; and when you awake, they will talk to you." (NKJV) That is to say that the Word is your sure guide for victory and permanent success.

I'll never forget what God impressed in my spirit a long time ago. He said to me, "if you would abide in My Word, the world would be nothing before you." In other words, with the Word, I can rule and reign in this world with ease. That's the God-life! I urge you today, don't stop with just listening to the Word or studying the Word, you must confess it as well. Confess that Christ's sufficiency is your sufficiency. Confess that greater is He that dwells on the inside of you than the calamities, devils, and troubles of the world. Say with confidence that you rule and reign in this world by Christ's sufficiency that works in you. So, do not lose your inspiration. God has greater things He wants to accomplish in you and through you.

Faith-Filled Confession:
The Greater One lives on the inside of me; I will not be moved or afraid. I enjoy peace and joy. The Word of God is my sure guide and assurance. I am strengthened to do the supernatural and to manifest all that God has put in me. In Jesus' name, Amen.

love

Saints, being steadfast in love is not an option for us
It's the only way for the believer in Jesus Christ to live

Communion

AGAPE LOVE

"For in Jesus Christ neither circumcision availeth anything,
nor uncircumcision; but faith which worketh by love".
(Galatians 5:6 KJV)

The hallmark of the believer in Jesus Christ is love.
And not just any kind of sensual love, but agape love: God's kind
of love. Jesus said in John 13:35 (KJV), "By this shall all *men* know
that ye are my disciples if ye have love one to another." And in
the preceding verse, He tells us just how: "Love one another. As
I have loved you, so you must love one another." (NIV) In other
words, if you profess to be a Christian, and do not demonstrate
love, you are in great error and are not true to your core identity.
Jesus' command was not for us to only love those that look like us
or act like us. He commanded that we love everybody in the same
manner that He loved us – flaws and all. "...God demonstrates His
own love for us in this: While we were still sinners, Christ died for
us." (Romans 5:8 NIV)

By the Spirit, the Apostle Paul wrote in 1 Corinthians 13:1-6
(NKJV): "Though I speak with the tongues of men and of angels,
but have not love, I have become sounding brass or a clanging
cymbal. And though I have *the gift of* prophecy, and understand
all mysteries and all knowledge, and though I have all faith, so that
I could remove mountains, but have not love, I am nothing. And
though I bestow all my goods to feed *the poor,* and though I give
my body to be burned, but have not love, it profits me nothing."
So, I can rightly say that love is a symbol of Christianity. You may
not approve of an individual's behavior or actions, but you must
always love the person. And until we fix the issue of love, we will
not manifest the fullness of all that God has for us.

Yes, as a Christian, we have been called into a life of eternal victory.
Christ already paid the price for us to live each day in prosperity,
health and victory. Yet, so many believers still live lives that are void
of victory. Many times, it is not because they lack faith. Often times,
it is due to them not walking in love towards others. Galatians 5:6

tells us that the only way faith can work is by love; so, no love, no effective faith. And faith is the way to receive from God.

Saints, you need your faith to be effective to enjoy all that is yours in Christ. Harboring unforgiveness and bitterness towards anyone is like drinking poison in the hopes that the other person dies. It's not worth it! It is pure cancer that hinders you from enjoying all that Christ has for you. Do not believe the lie that there are certain people you cannot love. As a believer, you have the nature of God, which is the nature of love and there is no person in this world that you cannot love. The love of God has been shared abroad in your heart by the Holy Ghost (Romans 5:5). 1 John 4:7-11 (NKJV) puts it this way: "Beloved, let us love one another, for love is of God; and everyone who loves is born of God and knows God. He who does not love does not know God, for God is love. In this the love of God was manifested toward us, that God has sent His only begotten Son into the world, that we might live through Him. In this is love, not that we loved God, but that He loved us and sent His Son *to be* the propitiation for our sins. Beloved, if God so loved us, we also ought to love one another."

Saints, you must be intentional about walking in love and be diligent in demonstrating the love of God towards others.

Faith-Filled Confession:
I am born of God and therefore, I am born of love. I have the nature of love because I have the nature of God. I demonstrate God's love to everyone. I refuse to be easily offended. I forgive quickly and completely because of the ability of Christ working in me.

EXPRESS LOVE

"Beloved, let us love one another, for love is from God; and everyone who loves is born of God and knows God."
(1 John 4:7 NKJV)

Love is who we are. Jesus said, "By this shall all men know that ye are my disciples if ye have love one to another." (John 13:35 KJV) Love is who the Christian is. The Christian is wired with God's liquid love and as a result, has no problem walking in love. The Christian has the life and the nature of God which is love. See, God does not just have love, He is love, and as a Christian, you are the reproduction of love. That's big! So, not only do you have love, but you have the ability to demonstrate love. And this is one reason why you must embrace the ministry of the Spirit in your life. The Holy Spirit will not only teach you to love, but He will also cause you to love just like the Father loves. Praise God!

To embrace love is to embrace healing, prosperity, transformation, growth, progress, success, and all that grace has made available to you in Christ. To embrace love is to yield to your divine nature. So awake to your divinity, and pour forth Christ's liquid love to others irrespective of their actions and inactions. It is the giving of oneself without any reservation just as Christ gave Himself to you. Jesus said, "Love one another. As I have loved you, so you also must love one another." (John 13:34 BSB) When you awake to your divinity, love and healing will flow in your life. This is something that many of God's people are ignorant of. I remember a story a Pastor friend shared with me about a sister in his church, who was diagnosed with cancer. As the pastor prayed with her, the Lord revealed to him that the cause of the cancer was bitterness and unforgiveness. The pastor told her that she needed to forgive and embrace love and joy, which she did. A couple of weeks later, she began to experience improvement in her health and it appeared that the cancer had gone into remission. Just when you would have thought that she would be more purposeful about walking in love, she picked up a quarrel with another person and got herself again into the bandwagon of unforgiveness. It wasn't long after that, that the cancer came back aggressively and eventually took her life. It was a painful loss to the church and her family. It would surprise you to know how many of God's people have been crushed because they failed to embrace their divine nature of love. Not embracing your divinity means that you are already in a losing battle against adverse circumstances and devils of darkness, because without love your faith is useless (Galatians 5:6).

James 3:16 (KJV) says, "For where envying and strife is, there is confusion and every evil work." The presence of envy and strife is a sign that one has not awoken to his or her divinity. And the presence of confusion and every evil work means that success, progress, and prosperity will not come to light in the life of the one that is walking in envy and strife. So, when we talk about walking in love, it is more than you trying to get along with those you perceive to be difficult in your life. Rather, it is proof that you are born of God. Remember, we are not talking about loving your neighbor as yourself; instead, we are talking about loving others as Christ loves you.

As a born-again believer in Jesus Christ, you have a charge to demonstrate the liquid love of Christ to your family members, neighbors, co-workers, and even to strangers. They must be able to see it and drink of it whenever they make contact with you. So, today, choose to be a love well that others can draw from.

Faith-Filled Confession:
I am full of the love of God. Therefore, I refuse to walk in unforgiveness, strife, envy or bitterness. I reject any tendency to be judgmental. I refuse to speak ill of others regardless of what they do or say. I forgive easily and dispense grace everywhere I go.

LOVE ALL THE WAY

"Be perfect, therefore, as your Heavenly Father is perfect."
(Matthew 5:48 NIV)

Jesus said, "You have heard that it was said, 'Love your neighbor and hate your enemy.' But I tell you, love your enemies and pray for those who persecute you, that you may be sons of your Father in heaven." (Matthew 5:43-45 NKJV) The expression "that you may be sons of your Father," is to buttress the truth that when we walk in love, we produce, unveil, and reveal the miraculous power of God which is associated with those born of Him. It takes love to communicate Christ effectively. Love is like a catalyst that causes the divine life in you to explode. It enables those around you to encounter Jesus in a marvelous and special way. God is all that He is because He is love. I would to God you caught this! The very essence of God is love. There is no God without love and there is no love without God. 1 John 4:8 (NIV) says "...God is love." And 1 Corinthians 13:8 (NIV) says "Love never fails..." In other words, love which is God, never fails; it does not bow to any situation. 1 John 5:4 says faith is the victory that overcomes the world and Galatians 5:6 says faith works by love. So, if faith gives you the victory, walking in love will make you master and lord. Love gives you dominion over every contradiction that the world or Satan may throw at you. The one who walks in love by default is Satan's worst nightmare because when you walk in love, you operate from the essence of God and by so doing, you unleash all of God's power.

Paul the apostle had this understanding and this is why he prayed for the church at Ephesus saying, "And I pray that you, being rooted and grounded in love, may have power, together with all the saints, to comprehend the length and width and height and depth of His love, and to know the love of Christ that surpasses knowledge, that you may be filled with all the fullness of God." (Ephesians 3:18-19 ESV) I have also observed that those who have experienced the unprecedented power of the Holy Spirit had one thing in common – love for people. Child of God, walking

87

in unconditional love is the only way for us. We cannot afford to do otherwise.

People may be rude, but stay in love and be kind to them. Do not allow anything or anyone to short-change this unspeakable grace for supernatural accomplishments in your life. So, you must prioritize the Word over everything else. Hell may throw everything at you to distract your mind from walking in love, but be sure to keep your thoughts on God's Word. Resist even unto blood every tendency to walk in offense. Stay ahead by forgiving others in advance. LOVE IS THE WAY!

Faith-Filled Confession:
Thank You, Father, that I am rooted and grounded in love, and I have received the power, together with all the saints, to comprehend the length and width and height and depth of Your love, and I have come to know the love of Christ that surpasses knowledge; hence, I am filled with all the fullness of God. Amen (Ephesians 3:18-19).

EMBRACE HIS LOVE

"But go, tell His disciples and Peter, 'He is going ahead of you into Galilee. There you will see Him, just as He told you.'" (Mark 16:7 NIV)

There may have been times when you allowed yourself to get overwhelmed by the circumstance of the moment. Maybe it was because you didn't like the way you were treated, or because things didn't quite go your way like you thought they should have. And so, you allowed your mind to imagine the worst possible scenarios. Then you got angry; not only at yourself but also at everyone involved. However, after looking back, you realize that you were wrong about the whole thing and that you had blown things out of proportion. Rather than give others the benefit of the doubt, you rushed to a conclusion that presented them in a negative light. If you can connect with this or have been here before, you are not alone. Peter, the Apostle, blew it too just like so many of us have. But God's mercy and grace remained unrelenting. Aren't you glad that God judges us with grace? He sees us through the finished work of Jesus and not through the imperfection of our works. Hallelujah!

If there was anyone that thought that they didn't deserve a second chance, it was Peter. He implied that in his response to Jesus when Jesus said, "I tell you the truth, Peter—this very night before the rooster crows, you will deny three times that you even know Me." (Matthew 26:34 NLT) Peter said to Jesus, "Even if I must die with You, I will never deny You." (Matthew 26:35 WEB) But when the time came, Peter did exactly as Jesus had described. And when it happened, "The Lord turned and looked straight at Peter. Then Peter remembered the Word the Lord had spoken to him: "Before the rooster crows today, you will disown me three times." (Luke 22:61 NIV) You should have seen the face of Peter that day. The bible says that "...he went outside and wept bitterly." (Luke 22:62 NIV)

Peter was so disappointed in himself that he abandoned the other disciples to go back to his fishing business. But when the Lord arose from the dead, the angel that was standing by the tomb said specifically, "But go, tell His disciples and Peter, 'He is going ahead of you into Galilee. There you will see him, just as he told you.'" (Mark 16:7 NIV) In other words, the message to Peter was to remind Peter that he was still one of Jesus' disciples. The message was to tell Peter that the Lord was not holding anything against him and that he was loved, just as much as the others who didn't deny Him.

What did Peter do when he heard those precious words? He yielded to the love and mercy of Jesus. Saints, whatever mistake you may have made in the past, is in the past; you can't take it back. However, there is something more powerful than your mistake, and it is your acceptance of His love. Peter embraced the mercy and love of Jesus and ended up becoming the great Apostle Peter who led the church and wrought great miracles in the name of the same Jesus whom he once denied three times. If Peter found hope, restoration, and purpose in the mercy and love of Jesus, I believe there is hope, restoration, and purpose for you today as well. Embrace the love of Jesus.

Faith-Filled Confession:
Nothing can separate me from the love of Christ for I am rooted and grounded in His love. I am assured of His love for me. He will never leave me nor forsake me. I am never alone. Hallelujah!

HAVE FAITH IN THE FATHER'S LOVE

"I'm sure now I'll see God's goodness in the exuberant earth. Stay with God! Take heart. Don't quit. I'll say it again: Stay with God." (Psalm 27:14 MSG)

Have faith in God's love for you and let your faith in His love propel you. Let nothing suggest to you that you are not loved, or that there is something wrong with you. Child of God, there is nothing wrong with you. You are God's choice and will forever be His choice. So, have faith in His love. You may be reading this, and you are wondering, "If indeed I am God's choice, why are things the way that they are for me? Things seem to be working for others but not for me." Child of God, God has no favorites in His family; not even Jesus is the Father's favorite. Jesus once held the position of being the Father's favorite, and this when He still had the position of being the only begotten of the Father. However, after He was raised from the dead, He became the first begotten of the Father, and because you are also begotten of the Father, the Father loves you just like He loves Jesus. Jesus put it this way in John 16:26-27: "In that day you will ask in My name. I am not saying that I will ask the Father on your behalf. No, the Father Himself loves you because you have loved Me and have believed that I came from God." (John 16:26-27 NIV) Notice the expression, "the Father Himself loves you."

I said that to say this: God does not choose who wins and who loses. In His family, we are all winners. He has given to each one of us the same eternal life, the same Word of God, and the same Holy Ghost. It is now up to each person to prove the Word for themselves. If one is prospering and another isn't, it is not because God chose for it to be so. Hebrews 4:2 (KJV) says, "For unto us was the gospel preached, as well as unto them: but the word preached did not profit them, not being mixed with faith in them that heard it." In other words, what we do with what God has given to us, determines the quality of our lives.

If things are already looking like they are going to be difficult, I have good news for you: they will not be difficult. The Lord said something to me that blessed me so much and I believe it will bless you too. He said, "Just because things appear to be a certain way, doesn't make them so. It only becomes that way when you endorse it with your confession." Then, He said, "the power of your circumstance is in your mouth." I lend you these words today. You are going to record BIG WINS! Just have faith in the Father's love for you. Don't wish to have the life of someone else. God has something special for you. Seize the Word that He has placed before you.

Remember that you are God's choice. All is well! "...stay with God! Take heart. Don't quit. I'll say it again: Stay with God." (Psalm 27:14 MSG)

Faith-Filled Confession:
Nothing can separate me from the love of Christ for I am rooted and grounded in His love. I am assured of His love for me. He will never leave me nor forsake me. I am never alone. Hallelujah!

WALKING IN LOVE IS SUBMITTING TO GOD

"If you love Me, keep My commands." (John 14:15 NIV)

Jesus said in John 13:35 (NIV), "By this everyone will know that you are My disciples if you love one another." In other words, the true and authentic way to demonstrate that you belong to Jesus is not by prophecies, healing, casting out devils, speaking in tongues or any other manifestation of the Spirit. The way to show that you truly belong to Jesus is by walking in love. Paul said in 1 Corinthians 12:3 (AMP), "If I had the gift of prophecy, and if I understood all of God's secret plans and possessed all knowledge, and if I had such faith that I could move mountains, but didn't love others, I would be nothing." That is to say, that a true and consistent life of the miraculous is rooted in walking in love. It is possible for anyone to occasionally experience the supernatural manifestation of the power of God without walking in love; however, it is impossible to consistently experience that power without walking in love. Prophecies, tongues, casting out of devils and moving in the spirit mean nothing before God if they do not come from a place of love. Your love walk is of utmost importance to God. Remember what Jesus said in Matthew 7:22-23 (NIV), "Many will say to Me on that day, 'Lord, Lord, did we not prophesy in Your name and in Your name drive out demons and, in Your name, perform many miracles?' "And then I will declare to them, 'I never knew you; DEPART FROM ME, YOU WHO PRACTICE LAWLESSNESS." These ones will be told to depart from the Lord because their activities, though spiritual, were void of love. John the Apostle wrote in 1 John 4:20 (NIV), "Whoever claims to love God yet hates a brother or sister is a liar. For whoever does not love their brother and sister, whom they have seen, cannot love God, whom they have not seen." And when you read 1 John 3:15 (NIV) you see just how serious walking in love is to God. John the Apostle said, "Anyone who hates a brother or sister is a murderer, and you know that no murderer has eternal life residing in him."

Irrespective of what others have said about you, or done to you, you have a duty to WALK IN LOVE. Remember, you are the light of the world and you have no acceptable excuse for failing to walk in love. There will always be mean people who will say hateful things. Yet, you must learn to live above the darkness of this world. Yes! There will be unfair treatments like you have never experienced before; still, you must be the light and let your light shine; love fuels your shine.

"Pastor, you ought to have heard what she said about me." Child of God, it doesn't matter. The most important thing is how you respond. Think of it this way: God is doing great things in your life, but there is an adversary who is angry to see things shift for your good. His only option is to distract you from what God is doing right now. Child of God, as long as you are focused on God's divine grace at work in you, he remains limited and inconsequential. But the moment you take your eyes away, he will pounce on you. What does he do? He stirs up trouble wherever or whenever he can. However, you must keep him in his place of defeat and hopelessness. You must continue to submit to God by walking in love toward everyone.

Faith-Filled Confession:
I am born of love because I am born of God. I do not struggle to love as Jesus loved. It comes from the depth of my being. And if anyone has offended me, I forgive them.

DON'T BE WEARY IN LOVE

"For in Jesus Christ neither circumcision availeth anything, nor uncircumcision; but faith which worketh by love."
(Galatians 5:6 KJV)

Speaking in tongues, casting out devils, and every other manifestation of the Spirit is meaningless before God if love is absent. The most important thing to God is your love walk. Remember what Jesus said in Matthew 7:22-23 (NIV). He said, "Many will say to Me on that day, 'Lord, Lord, did we not prophesy in Your name and in Your name drive out demons and, in Your name, perform many miracles?' "And then I will declare to them, 'I never knew you; DEPART FROM ME, YOU WHO PRACTICE LAWLESSNESS." Why would Jesus tell these ones to depart from Him? It is because they did all that they did without love. John the Apostle put it so succinctly in 1 John 4:20 (NIV) when he said, "Whoever claims to love God yet hates a brother or sister is a liar. For whoever does not love their brother and sister, whom they have seen, cannot love God, whom they have not seen."

Like I have always said; regardless of what others may do to you, or say about you, YOU MUST WALK IN LOVE. Remember that you are the light of the world. There is no valid excuse for walking outside of love. You can't participate in any form of gossip about your boss, roommate, colleague, or anyone else for that matter even if they've warranted it by their actions. Yes! People will be mean and hateful, but you are to live above the darkness of this world. Yes! There will be unfair treatments like you have never experienced before, but you must be the light, and your light only shines when you walk in love.

Jesus was never caught off guard. Regardless of what was said or done to Him, He maintained His spiritual cool; not because He didn't feel the pain of betrayal or insults from others, but because He understood that functioning outside of love leaves one exposed to satanic attacks and manipulations. In 2 Corinthians 2:10-11 (BSB), Paul the Apostle said this: "If you forgive anyone, I also forgive him. And if I have forgiven anything, I have forgiven it in the presence of Christ for your sake, so that Satan should not outwit us. For we are not unaware of his schemes." He connected unforgiveness to being outwitted by Satan.

Unforgiveness is a strategy of the enemy. He wants us to be so provoked by how we are treated by others to the point where we become nonchalant about walking in love. I'll say it again; regardless of what may have been said or done to you, you must respond in love.

Faith-Filled Confession:
I am born of God. Therefore, I am born of love. I refuse to harbor unforgiveness; I forgive quickly and completely. God's love flows in me and through me. I refuse to give a foothold to the adversary. The schemes of the adversary concerning me and my family are frustrated and paralyzed in the name of Jesus, Amen. (1 John 4:7, 2 Cor 2:10-11).

WALK IN LOVE AND YOU WILL WALK IN THE FULLNESS

"Everything God does is right— the trademark on all His works is love." (Psalm 145:17 MSG)

In Ephesians 3:19 (NIV), Apostle Paul prayed that the church at Ephesus would "know this love that surpasses knowledge—that they may be filled to the measure of all the fullness of God," because our comprehension of the love of God determines how well we walk in the fullness of God. In 1 John 4:16 (NIV), we see that "...God is love [and] whoever lives in love lives in God, and God in them." It is impossible to know God this way and not walk in His fullness or manifest the totality of His being, to the extent where anyone who encounters you, encounters God, and their lives are forever changed by the presence of God in you. Psalm 145:17 (MSG) says, "Everything God does is right— the trademark on all His works is love." In this season, we have received a grace and an anointing that has the trademark of God's love. And this anointing can only be effective by love - love that is based on the Word and motivated by the Word.

Do not be shocked when people grow cold on you; they suddenly go from warm to ice cold. Also, do not blame them for their behavior. It's all the enemy's attempt to sway you away from your position in Christ. Instead of reacting to what they said or did, just do what Jesus would do if He was in your shoes. I have often said that the way people treat us is not our business. The way we are treated cannot cause a short-circuit in the flow of the anointing for spreading that is upon our lives. On the other hand, the way we respond can. By walking in bitterness or unforgiveness, we can hinder the flow of grace. So, let's focus on that which is our responsibility - walk in unconditional love. Remember Jesus' words in John 14:15 (NIV): "If you love Me, keep My commands." And when we keep His Word, we demonstrate faith.

Child of God, be sure to live a life of love; treat others like you would Jesus. Their actions may not always meet your expectations but you must learn to see them through the lens of Love. And if there are those whose actions consistently fall short of your expectations, Colossians 3:13 MSG says, "Be even-tempered, content with second place, quick to forgive an offense. Forgive as quickly and completely as the Master forgave you."

My prayer for you today is that you will always be motivated by God's Word to walk in love even when there are strong logical reasons to do otherwise. As you do the Word, I pray that you will continue to experience the fullness of God's grace to spread abroad in every direction.

Faith-Filled Confession:
My faith is effective because I walk in love. I choose to love others in the same manner that Christ loved me. His love flows through me today to everyone that comes in contact with me, in Jesus' name, Amen. (John 13:34; Galatians 5:6)

AN ICON OF LOVE AND
COMPASSION OF CHRIST

"Let brotherly love continue. Do not neglect to show hospitality to strangers, for thereby some have entertained angels unawares. Remember those who are in prison, as though in prison with them, and those who are mistreated, since you also are in the body." (Hebrews 13:1-3 ESV)

You will hardly find a man or woman who walks in unconditional love get sick or broke; their lives are forever a display of the reality of Christ. It's not as though they do not face the same challenges that others encounter, but when they do, their faith prevails. They have greater testimonies and tend to manifest the blessings of God in a greater way. If you have read the Scriptures like I have, you would agree with me that there is no place in the Book where darkness prevailed over light. The reverse is always the case; light comes, and darkness instantly disappears without an argument. Love is the same way. There is nothing in heaven, on earth, or in hell that can outlive love. Love is first and last; everything else will come and go but love abides forever. Love is a divine weapon given to us by God to experience mind-boggling testimonies. Those who walk in unconditional love are mountain movers, planet shakers, and a nightmare to hell. What may take others days or even months to accomplish, takes them a fraction of the time.

Jesus was a prime example of one who displayed unconditional love and was a living, walking wonder in the earth. Some may say, "He was Jesus! What would you have expected?" But you must remember that Jesus did not live the way He did because He was God. He functioned as a man in this world to demonstrate to us what was possible as children of God. He is an example of what is possible when you have the life of God in you. So now that this life is on the inside of you, heaven does not expect anything less. Hence Philippians 2:5-8 (NKJV) says, "Let this mind be in you which was also in Christ Jesus, who, being in the form of God, did not consider it robbery to be equal with God, but made Himself of no reputation, taking the form of a bondservant, and coming in the likeness of men. And being found in appearance as a man, He humbled Himself and became obedient to the point of death, even the death of the cross."

Not only does Heaven expect you to walk as a wonder in the earth like Jesus, but you are expected to do greater things than He did (John 14:12). And for that to be possible, you must have the mindset of unconditional love like Jesus. When you take a look at Jesus and the Christian today, you'll notice the lack of the glow of the supernatural which was commonplace with Jesus when He walked the face of the earth, and the obvious missing component is the display of unconditional love among many today.

Saints, being steadfast in love is not an option for us. It's the only way for the believer in Jesus Christ to live. So "Let brotherly love continue. Do not neglect to show hospitality to strangers, for thereby some have entertained angels unawares. Remember those who are in prison, as though in prison with them, and those who are mistreated, since you also are in the body." (Hebrews 13:1-3 ESV) We have the responsibility to show our world God's glory. Let the people in your world describe you as an icon of Christ's love and compassion.

Faith-Filled Confession:
As Christ is, so I am in this world. As Christ is love, so I am in this world. The love and compassion of God flows through me to everyone that I encounter today, in Jesus' name, Amen.

THE KEY IS LOVING JESUS

"Jesus replied, "If anyone loves Me, he will keep My word. My Father will love him, and we will come to him and make Our home with him." (John 14:23 NKJV)

Loving Jesus should be your strongest desire as a child of God, because you can't really say that you are living until you are in pursuit of what pleases Him. Ask yourself this question, "Am I living for God or am I living for myself?" And if the answer to that question is, "Yes, I am living for God." My follow up question would be, "How do you know?" Because simply saying that you are living for God does not mean that you are. What tells us whether or not you are living for God or that you love Him is the value that you place on His Word and your obedience to His instructions.

Saints, declaring your love for Jesus should be your number one priority in life. Jesus said in John 14:23 (NKJV), "If anyone loves Me, he will keep My Word." If we say that we truly love God, then we must allow His Word to be the driving force behind all that we do, even when His instructions may not make logical sense. At the wedding at Cana, Jesus asked His disciples to draw water out of cleansing pots to serve to the wedding guests (John 2). Now, just imagine the disciples of Jesus saying amongst themselves, "This is just wrong! It makes no sense! How can we draw water from these dirty pots and serve it to the Governor? I think someone should let the Master know that He misspoke." Sometimes God would speak directly to us through His Word or through our spiritual leaders, and there are times when His instructions sound ridiculous, yet we must treat them with utmost reverence and seek to obey Him to the letter. If the disciples had judged the instructions of God by their mental capacity, they would have missed out on such a great miracle. But thank God for Mary who had earlier instructed the disciples saying, "Whatever He tells you to do, do it."

Today, I am saying to you; do not rely on your senses. Your senses will fail you. Also, do not judge spiritual things by the wisdom of this world; it would only lead you down the road of destruction.

101

Proverbs 14:12 (KJV) says, "There is a way which seemeth right unto a man, but the end thereof are the ways of death." I have always said that popularity does not equal revelation. Hence, you must study the Word for yourself. Jesus made it so simple for us; He said, "If you love Me, just do what I say" (Nothing more and nothing less). In other words, each time you do God's Word, you declare your love for Jesus. And Jesus said to the one that does that, "My Father will love him, and we will come to him and make Our home with him." (John 14:23 NKJV) In other words, when this happens, God's power will be demonstrated.

Loving Jesus is KEY. When we demonstrate our love for Jesus by doing His word, we bring to light everything that God has said concerning us; our victory, health, wealth, increase is brought into manifestation.

Faith-Filled Confession:
I am an epistle of Christ Jesus and I demonstrate my love for Jesus by being an effective doer of His Word. In doing the Word, I showcase the glory, honor and virtues of Christ. My life is synonymous with miracles, signs and wonders. Hallelujah!

miracles

I am a supernatural being;
full of vitality and loaded with the miraculous working
power of God

BE KNOWLEDGEABLE ABOUT MIRACLES

"These miraculous signs will accompany those who believe: They will cast out demons in my name, and they will speak in new languages...They will be able to place their hands on the sick, and they will be healed." (Mark 16:17-18 NLT)

If there is one thing that the enemy dreads, it is a believer that knows and participates in the workings of miracles. In other words, a believer that walks in signs and wonders. Amazingly, everyone that is born again has been called into this glorious manifestation of God's grace and power; a life of continuous demonstration of notable miracles and victories. Jesus said these miraculous signs will characterize everyone that is born again. Can it get better than that? Imagine each one of us manifesting the fullness of this glorious life in Christ Jesus. Imagine what would happen to our cities. I can tell you one thing; our cities would not be the same again.

So why aren't believers walking in the authority that is in Christ Jesus? It is simply because most Christians have little knowledge or understanding about how to walk in the light of their salvation which includes walking in the authority that we have in the name of Jesus Christ. If as a Christian, you have never been taught on how to walk in the authority that is in the name of Jesus, chances are that you have been in the wrong assembly all your life. The authority of the believer should be a foundational teaching in every assembly, plain and simple. The idea that only a chosen few are to walk in the supernatural is a lie from the pit of hell. The description that Jesus gave of the one that is born again is nothing short of an icon of the miraculous. Did you ever read what Jesus said in John 14:12? He said, "Very truly I tell you, whoever believes in me will do the works I have been doing, and they will do even greater things than these because I am going to the Father." If this is true, then we have been short-changing ourselves of great opportunities that would have brought glory to our Heavenly Father.

Hear me! If anyone preaches another gospel other than what Jesus had said, let that person be accursed! If Jesus emphatically

105

stated that the Christian life is a life of great manifestation of notable miracles and victories, then we must refuse to settle for anything that suggests, sponsors or tolerates a life that is void of the supernatural. Just for the record, I fully understand that many have relinquished the supernatural to just walking in love and being nice to your coworkers and neighbors. Hear me loud and clear, anyone that is truly walking in love would demonstrate in unthinkable measures the miraculous signs and wonders of the Holy Spirit. In Ephesians 3:19 AMP the scriptures declare, "and [that you may come] to know [practically, through personal experience] the love of Christ which far surpasses [mere] knowledge [without experience], that you may be filled up [throughout your being] to all the fullness of God [so that you may have the richest experience of God's presence in your lives, completely filled and flooded with God Himself]. Saints of God, you can't be filled with all the fullness of God and be oppressed by the devil or allow those around you to be tormented by circumstances. The days of hiding behind religious clichés are long gone. You are a supernatural personality that is loaded with the power of the Holy Ghost. It's about time every devil in your neighborhood checked out! It is about time the sick around you got healed. Get your mind right; get it to focus on your supernatural personality and walk in the authority that is in the name of Jesus.

Be knowledgeable about the miracles of Jesus and whatever you see, do! Praise God! Be bold! Use the name of Jesus over every devil of darkness wherever you find them. And when you do, they would not be able to say no to you.

Faith-Filled Confession:
I have authority over every devil hatched out of hell, sickness, disease and every situation that does not accord to the reality of Christ and His triumph over hell and death. I am a supernatural personality with divine ability. I rule and dominate every device of the enemy. I put out darkness everywhere I go today. I refuse to negotiate with hatred, sickness, hopelessness, defeat, frustration or lack. In the name of the Lord Jesus Christ.

BE MINDFUL OF THE SUPERNATURAL

"Jesus answered them, is it not written in your law, I said, 'You are gods?' ... He called them gods, to whom the word of God came (and the Scripture cannot be broken)." (John 10:34,35 NKJV)

If there is one thing you must consciously reject, it is the idea that the Christian is not really who the scriptures describe. You may have heard people make statements like, "no man is perfect." What they are saying in essence is that everybody is a mess. Sometimes you have to discern when someone is trying to make up for their spiritual bankruptcy. Just because you heard a "preacher" say that "no one is perfect" or that "we are all miserable and in need of a savior," does not mean that they are speaking the Word of God. Before you got born again, you were miserable and in need of a savior. However, after salvation you can no longer talk that way. Such a statement is an error that denies the work of the Lordship of Jesus in your life. Now that you are in Christ, you are no longer a mess. The Bible declares that you have been made complete in Christ... (Colossians 2:10).

In John 10:34-35, Jesus said something very profound. He said, it is written in the scriptures (quoting Himself); "I said you are gods." Wait a minute! Who? Me? Then He goes further to say that those to whom the Word of God came, they were called gods. In other words, when the Word of God comes to a man, it makes that man more than a man. It makes that man supernatural. The Word of God comes to you fully packed with abilities, causing you to defy natural courses. When the Word came to Peter, the Word caused Peter to walk on water defying the natural law of gravity (Matthew 14:29). When the Word came to Jeremiah, Jeremiah saw himself as a youth that was too young to bear the message of God, but the Word came to correct the wrong perception and to re-align him to the very purpose for which He was born; to be a prophet to the nations (Jeremiah 1: 4-8). The Word of God came to Moses, and made him a god unto pharaoh (Exodus 7:1). Throughout the scriptures we see how the Word made gods out of men, causing them to defy natural laws and progressions. We also see how the Word came to contrary situations, sicknesses, lack and even death and caused the supernatural to happen! In Jesus' dealing with the fig tree in Mark 11, the Word came to the fig tree and caused it to dry up from its roots.

When Jesus asked the question, "Is it not written in your law, I said, 'You are gods?'" He was actually quoting Himself from Psalm 82:7-8 (NKJV); "I said, "You are gods, and all of you are children of the Most High. But you shall die like men, and fall like one of the princes." Why would He say so? Because if you do not know who are and what you have, chances are that you would live and die like mere men who are controlled by the externals and tossed to and from by whatever moves. In other words, if a Christian lacks understanding of their identity in Christ, their life would look identical to one who is not saved.

For this reason, it is of utmost importance that you befriend God's Word. Set out time to study the Bible for yourself. The Psalmist declared; "the entrance of thy words giveth light; it giveth understanding unto the simple." (Psalm 119:130 KJV) Allow the Word of God "come" to you and better still, "enter" into you. Each time the Word comes to you for a particular area, it comes with the ability to make you supernatural in that area. Let the Word gain entrance into your heart, your mind and body. Do not put a guard on the Word. Allow it to illuminate, transform and direct you in all that you do. Remember, you are a god here on earth, and you have been called to display the miraculous power of God to your world. God bless you!

Faith-Filled Confession:
I am a supernatural being; full of vitality and loaded with the miraculous working power of God. I am born of the Word of God and my life displays the glory of the Word. I am diligent to study and understand God's Word and bold to share it with others. Today, I declare that I walk in miracles, signs and wonders. I defy natural laws and progressions to the glory of God! Hallelujah!

SET THE TIME FOR YOUR MIRACLE

"For she was saying to herself, "If I only touch His garment, I will get well." (Matthew 9:21 NASB)

One of the most beautiful things about the Christian life is the ability to determine the quality of your life. You can determine whether you are going to live life as a victor over sickness, poverty, hell and death or live a life of misery, frustration, sickness, lack and defeat. God is not going to make this decision for you. Neither is Satan equipped enough to stop you from living the life of glory if that is what you have chosen. The idea that if God wants me to have it, I will have it, does not apply to everything. There are things that are a result of the sovereignty of God and there are others that are within the sovereignty of your own faith. If you're thinking, "what shall be, shall be," it means that you have short-changed yourself for the most part. Chances are that you have not been living the life of a victor that Christ died for you to have.

For example, the rapture of the church is outside of your sovereignty. Therefore, it doesn't matter how much you pray for it not to happen, it will still happen. And praying that it happens in a given year will not work either. Jesus said, "But of that day and hour knoweth no man, no, not the angels of heaven, but my Father only." (Matthew 24:36 KJV) But when it comes to the things that grace has made available in Christ Jesus for you, they are no longer under the sovereignty of God but under the sovereignty of your faith. When it comes to your prosperity, health, joy, peace and victory, it is no longer a subject of if God wants me to have this or that then I will. Saying so is simply ignorance gone on rampage. Hear me, the will of God is already established in Christ Jesus concerning you. SO SET THE TIME FOR YOUR MIRACLE. God's will is wealth, healing, victory, success and all that grace has made available in Christ. So quit debating whether or not God wants you well and prosperous.

As you study the scriptures, you would find time and time again men and women who set the time for their miracles. They knew how to release their faith for a miracle. The woman with the issue of blood is a classic example. She could have complained and resolved to religious clichés like: "I guess God wants me to have this sickness" or "God is trying to teach me a lesson." Think about it. She was not the only one with this disease. Others in the same condition may have looked at the odds and history and thrown in the towel but not this woman! She heard that there was one called Jesus who was performing miracles and healings and that was all that she needed to hear. The Bible says that she kept talking to herself about how she was going to receive a miracle from Jesus. When others were hoping for a prayer to be said over them, she was saying to herself, "If I only touch His garment, I will get well." (Matthew 9:21 NASB) In other words, I don't need Him to pray or lay His hands on me, because it may never happen. She knew the odds that were mounting against her. But she just kept saying to herself, "If I only touch His garment, I will get well." Her faith had already set the time for that miracle and nothing was going to stop it from happening. And when that time came not only did she get healed of the issue of blood, she was made whole. Jesus said to her, "Daughter, thy faith hath made thee whole; go in peace, and be whole of thy plague." (Mark 5:34 KJV)

What am I telling you today? Wait no more! Refuse to hide behind religious walls. Set the time for your miracle today. The will of God in Christ Jesus concerning you is already A RESOUNDING YES! For the scripture declares; "For all of God's promises have been fulfilled in Christ with a resounding 'Yes!' And through Christ, our 'Amen' (which means 'Yes') ascends to God for His glory." (2 Corinthians 1:20 NLT)

Faith-Filled Confession:
I have testimonies of extraordinary, unthinkable and unspeakable miracles and victories. God's will for me is prosperity, victories, signs, wonders, progress and health and in the name of the Lord Jesus Christ, I take all that grace has supplied! I declare that there is peace, love and health for everyone that comes in contact with me today. This is my day of miracles. In Jesus mighty name. Amen! Hallelujah!

HEALING IS YOUR RIGHT

And ought not this woman, being a daughter of Abraham, whom Satan hath bound, lo, these eighteen years, be loosed from this bond on the Sabbath day? (Luke 13:16 KJV)

The fundamental of our faith lies in our understanding of what grace has been made available to us in Christ Jesus. So many of God's people can't tell the difference between a promise and a right and that I believe can be credited to the lack of firepower that is being demonstrated by many today, especially in their health and finances. For the most part, we pray for things that already belong to us or we ask God to do something for us that He told us to do. And this attitude is what cripples your faith. For example, you can pray from today till the rapture of the church about how Jesus should come and save the world; the only thing you will get would be a headache and unbelief because such a prayer does not account for faith. In Romans 10:6- 9 (NKJV) the Bible says, "But the righteousness of faith speaks in this way, "Do not say in your heart, 'Who will ascend into heaven?'" (that is, to bring Christ down from above) or, "'Who will descend into the abyss?'" (that is, to bring Christ up from the dead). But what does it say? "The word is near you, in your mouth and in your heart" (that is, the word of faith which we preach): that if you confess with your mouth the Lord Jesus and believe in your heart that God has raised Him from the dead, you will be saved." In other words, it's a done deal! And all you have to do is to endorse it to be so in your life. This means that every human soul has been granted the right to salvation; it's now their responsibility to either exercise this right and get born again or refuse the free gift of God and go to hell. Either way, the choice lies with us. And how is this right exercised? It is simply by believing in the Word. That is why John 1:12 (BSB) declares, "But to all who did receive Him, to those who believed in His name, He gave the right to become children of God." Hallelujah!

Think for a moment about the woman that was bent over whom Satan had afflicted for eighteen years in Luke 13:16; who also happened to be the daughter of Abraham. She was ignorant of the fact that her covenant right prohibited her from being afflicted by an evil spirit, and because of her ignorance, she suffered for eighteen long years! I guess some may argue, "Why didn't God do something before she encountered Jesus?" The answer is pure and simple; God will never do for you what He has already done. As a daughter of Abraham, it was her responsibility to exercise the right that was contained in the covenant that God had with Abraham. The reason for her suffering for eighteen long years was her failure to exercise her right over sickness and disease. The same is true today with many of God's people. They suffer not because God wants them to suffer but because of the very same reason that this daughter of Abraham suffered – ignorance of rights.

Listen! Jesus died, was buried and rose up again and all of that was not for nothing. The Bible declares that Papa God intentionally made Him (Jesus) sick for the sole purpose of making you well. Isaiah 53:10 (ESV) says, "Yet it was the will of the Lord to bruise Him; He has put Him to grief and made Him sick." Because of what Jesus did, healing is no longer a promise to those who are born again. It has become an inherent right; which means that the responsibility is now yours to refuse the advances of sickness and disease. But as long as you see healing as a promise, you will never walk in divine health. Divine health is your right! Take it! Praise God!

Faith-Filled Confession:
The life and the nature of God are at work in me. Good health is my right in Jesus Christ. I refuse to accommodate sickness or disease in my body. I am healed and living in divine health right now. I am whole in my body, my mind and my spirit! I declare that nothing fails in me and nothing fails around me. In the name of the Lord Jesus.

LOVE – THE SECRET TO THE MIRACULOUS

"If I had the gift of prophecy, and if I understood all of God's secret plans and possessed all knowledge, and if I had such faith that I could move mountains, but didn't love others, I would be nothing." (1 Corinthians 13:2 AMP)

Galatians 5:6 (KJV) says "For in Jesus Christ neither circumcision availeth any thing, nor uncircumcision; but faith which worketh by love." Faith makes love effective. The faith of one who does not walk in love is not real faith, and because it's not rooted in love, such faith will not produce the supernatural. If love fuels faith, love must also be the fuel for every other ministry of the Spirit. Paul alluded to this in 1 Corinthians 13:2 (NLT) when he said: "If I had the gift of prophecy, and if I understood all of God's secret plans and possessed all knowledge, and if I had such faith that I could move mountains but didn't love others, I would be nothing."

To walk in love, you must first believe and receive the love that God has for you. Jesus said in John 13:34 (NIV), "A new command I give you: love one another. As I have loved you, so you must love one another." Note that Jesus didn't say we should love others as we love ourselves; rather, He said we should love others as He loves us. The question is this: if you don't know or haven't received Christ's love for you, how then can you love someone else with the love of Christ? It's absolutely impossible! Because you can only give what you have, and until you start walking in love the way Christ walked in love, the supernatural life will be a mystery to you. Paul the apostle understood the power of knowing and walking in love. In his prayer for the church at Ephesus, he said, "and to know this love that surpasses knowledge—that you may be filled to the measure of all the fullness of God." (Ephesians 3:19 NIV) In other words, the fullness of God is predicated on knowing the love of Christ. There is nothing that hinders the ability of the adversary like a Christian who knows Christ's love and walks in it.

Say this: "I know that God loves me with an eternal love because He proved it by the sacrifice of His son Jesus. I know that God is thinking of me right at this moment. I know that God is working everything together for my good. I know that God is more interested in my success than I could ever be. I know that God's will for me is prosperity and health. And I declare that the expectation of the wicked, naysayers and the flesh have been pulverized by the anointing of God. I live an excellent life. I am an oasis of kindness and love to my world. I am victorious over all that is negative. I am not a needy person because God has already supplied all of my needs according to His riches in glory by Christ Jesus."

Child of God, you are an excellent, brilliant, and a great person to be around. You are not broken or miserable. You are God's righteousness and your name is synonymous with greatness. Romans 8:32 (NLT) says, "Since He did not spare even His own Son but gave Him up for us all, won't He also give us everything else?" Emphatically YES! The good news is that He already did. 1 Timothy 6:17 (NKJV) says God "...gives us richly all things to enjoy." Hallelujah! He did all of these and immeasurably more just to say to you, "I LOVE YOU." And since He has proven His love for you, you ought to allow others to experience this same love when they meet you. Serve them with excellence and reverence as you would Christ. Remember, there is no supernatural living without walking in love, especially towards those who have treated you wrongly.

A COLLAGE OF MIRACLES

"Moreover, the Word of the LORD came to me, saying, "Jeremiah, what do you see?" And I said, "I see a branch of an almond tree." Then the LORD said to me, "You have seen well, for I am ready to perform My Word." (Jeremiah 1:11-12 NKJV)

Facilitating the fulfillment of certain prophetic utterances sometimes in your life requires the use of visual aids. Today, I am not just referring to seeing things with the eyes of your heart; I am speaking of having physical representations of the words of prophecy that you have received set around you, at home or at your workplace.

These visual aids may be photos of things for which you are currently believing God or goals the Lord has placed in your heart to accomplish. For example, having a visual representation of a house that you are believing God for.

In Genesis 15:5, as the Lord began to affirm His plan for Abraham, who at the time couldn't imagine having a child with his wife, Sarah, God said, "Look now toward heaven, and count the stars if you are able to number them." And He said to him, "So shall your descendants be." I believe that God used the stars in the sky as a visual aid to help Abram imagine his descendants and exercise his faith.

The result, "He [Abraham] did not waver at the promise of God through unbelief, but was strengthened in faith, giving glory to God." In essence, that visual aid was enough connection for him to expect despite contrary conditions.

Saints, we serve a God whose greatest pleasure is to be believed. Take some time out during the day to make a list or collage of God's promises to you; the miracles you expect and the personal desires of your heart, as the Lord leads you. Put that list or collage of miracles in a place where your eyes will meet it every day and as you look at it, give God glory for the fulfillment. Get ready for an avalanche of miracles.

Faith-Filled Confession:
I am set on the path that I must follow; a path of peace, righteousness, and victory. My inheritance in Christ boggles human reasoning which is why I embrace the wisdom of God to bring to pass the uncommon in my life. And by these manifestations, many will come to know Jesus for the wonder He is. Hallelujah!

p e a c e

The presence of Jesus in you is peace, and this peace
does not bow to anything that is contrary to Christ
and His finished work

HAVE NO ANXIETY ABOUT ANYTHING

Trust God from the bottom of your heart; don't try to figure out everything on your own. Listen for God's voice in everything you do, everywhere you go; he's the one who will keep you on track. Don't assume that you know it all. (Proverbs 3:5-6 MSG)

Living the true Christian life is paramount to living

a worry-free life. Sadly, many of God's people are not living worry-free. They worry about their kids, spouse, bills, job, house and even about the weather! It appears as though they worry about everything, what a life! That's not what Jesus died for. John 10:10 NLT Jesus said, "My purpose is to give them a rich and satisfying life." and He has. So why are so many not living a rich and satisfying life? It is simply because of their unbelief. The word of God has not yet been unveiled to their heart. This is why the teaching of the word of God and the praying for the saints is so vital. Apostle Paul by the Spirit prayed for the Ephesians saints and in his prayer, he prayed, "open the eyes of their hearts, and let the light of Your truth flood in...." Ephesians 1:18 (VOICE)

He prayed that the saints grasp the immensity of this glorious way of life- the God Life - A life void of anxiety and worries. David said, "God, my shepherd! I don't need a thing. You have bedded me down in lush meadows, you find me quiet pools to drink from. True to your word, you let me catch my breath and send me in the right direction." Psalm 23:1-3 MSG Hallelujah!

Jesus said to Martha, "Martha! Martha! You are worried and bothered about so many things." In other words, Jesus said to Martha, seat down and let me take care of you. Maybe that is you today. Jesus is saying, "I got this! RELAX!"

Philippians 4:6 (VOICE) "Don't be anxious about things; instead, pray. Pray about everything. He longs to hear your requests, so talk to God about your needs and be thankful for what has come".

What you may not realize is that anxiety is pride and God resists the proud. 1 Peter 5:6-7 says "Humble yourselves therefore under the mighty hand of God, that he may exalt you in due time: casting all your care upon him; for he cares for you" Meaning, the way to humble yourself before the Lord is to cast all your anxiety upon him. Proverbs 3:5-6 (MSG) says, "Trust God from the bottom of your heart; don't try to figure out everything on your own. Listen for God's voice in everything you do, everywhere you go; he's the one who will keep you on track. Don't assume that you know it all."

Trust is not a gift. It is developed through relationship. Get into fellowship with the Father through His Word. Meditate on the word. Pray about everything and be thankful in every situation. As you do, your trust will grow and anxiety will dissipate. Praise God!

So, when you feel overwhelmed by adverse circumstances, practice waiting on Him with faith proclamations and see Him come through every time. His answer is always yes, and He is not a late God. Say this, "I have a rich and satisfying life void of anxiety." Praise God!

Faith-Filled Confession:
Everything about me is brought to perfection. I see possibilities and beauty in my life. I have a rich and satisfying life. My eyes are open and Your truth floods my thoughts today. I am anxious for nothing, in Jesus' name. Amen.

COMBAT ANXIETY WITH PEACE

"Peace I leave with you; My [own] peace I now give and bequeath to you. Not as the world gives do, I give to you. Do not let your hearts be troubled, neither let them be afraid. [Stop allowing yourselves to be agitated and disturbed; and do not permit yourselves to be fearful and intimidated and cowardly and unsettled]." (John 14:27 AMPC)

Contrary to what many have suggested, anxiety is not a normal part of life for the Christian. In the Kingdom of God, you do not have to experience down days. The wisdom of this world tells us: "You win sometimes and lose sometimes." However, the Kingdom of God has declared you to be a victor ever before you face any challenge. The world suggests that it is okay to be anxious when faced with challenges or uncertainties. The world sells fear and anxiety as acceptable commodities and oddly enough, many Christians have bought into this lie.

God wants you to experience peace. Peace is not the absence of trouble or challenges. Peace is based solely on God Himself, who is the same yesterday, today and forever. He sees the end from the beginning and has declared you to be victorious. Hallelujah! Romans 14:17 (KJV) says, "For the kingdom of God is...righteousness, peace, and joy in the Holy Ghost."

God has given us His life and His Spirit. 2 Timothy 1:7 (NKJV) clearly tells us that "God has not given us the spirit of fear; but of power, and of love, and of a sound mind." If He didn't give it to us, it means, we should not have it. If He didn't give you fear, it means it was never His design for you to experience fear or anxiety. The scriptures tell us that God has given us all things needed for a godly life (2 Peter 1:3), of which, fear was not included.

Science has tried for ages to explain why some people experience depression; if they had just consulted the Bible, that mystery could have long been solved. Proverbs 12:25 (NKJV) says, "Anxiety in the heart of man causes depression, but a good word makes it glad." If you let anxiety or fear dwell in your heart, it will cause depression and depression will ultimately make you a prey for Satan. When we examine the life of Job in the Bible, we see exactly where things went wrong for him. He said, "For the thing which I greatly feared has come upon me, and that which I was afraid of has come unto me." (Job 3:25 KJV) By operating in fear and anxiety, Job fell prey to Satan. Anxiety breaks the hedge and Ecclesiastes 10:8 (KJV) says, "...whoever breaketh a hedge, a serpent shall bite him."

John 14:27 (AMPC) Jesus said, "Peace I leave with you; My [own] peace I now give and bequeath to you." In other words, Jesus was letting us know that we have peace. Then He said "Not as the world gives do, I give to you." Revealing to us the quality of peace that He has given to us. He said His peace is different from the peace that the world may offer. The world offers a peace where you have to perform to get. The peace offered by the world is erratic and cannot be trusted. But Jesus has freely given us His peace and His peace does not change with the weather. His peace is constant. His peace is eternal. His peace is present even in the midst of chaos.

He went further to say, "Do not let your hearts be troubled, neither let them be afraid. [Stop allowing yourselves to be agitated and disturbed; and do not permit yourselves to be fearful and intimidated and cowardly and unsettled]." In other words, you have a part to play. It is your responsibility to not let your heart be troubled. It is your responsibility to not allow yourself to get agitated or disturbed. When thoughts of fear and anxiety come, do not permit them. Your mind and thoughts are the regulatory body for your body and spirit. You have the right to grant permits. If you grant a building permit to fear and anxiety, be assured to have a building as tall as the Eiffel tower constructed and when anxiety comes in, depression lies around the corner. You must cast down every thought and every imagination that is contrary to God's word in Christ concerning you and bring them to the obedience of Christ (2 Corinthians 10:5).

Jesus has given you peace and you must receive it by faith to have it operational. And when you have received His peace, confess, "I have the Peace of God." Meditate on the Word of God. Let His words frame your thoughts. Isaiah 26:3 (NLT) says "You will keep in perfect peace all who trust in you, all whose thoughts are fixed on you!"

Give no room to fear or anxiety! Just like Jesus said to Jairus in Luke chapter 8, STOP THE FEAR! Bombard your mind with His word and speak His word only and experience His peace that passeth understanding flood your heart.

Faith-Filled Confession:
Thank You Father for your joy and peace. I declare that I have peace on every side. I have peace in my mind, peace in my body, peace in my spirit, peace in my home, peace on my job, and in all that concerns me. My children are taught of the Lord and great is my peace. I endorse my victory. I give no room to fear or anxiety. I agree with God's word in Christ concerning me. I refuse to be regulated by the externals. I declare that I happen to my world today. In Jesus' name. Amen.

WORRY-FREE ZONE

"Trust God from the bottom of your heart; don't try to figure out everything on your own. Listen for God's voice in everything you do, everywhere you go; he's the one who will keep you on track. Don't assume that you know it all."
(Proverbs 3:5-6 MSG)

Every Christian is a wonder to this world. There is nothing ordinary about you. The life and the nature of God have been imparted into you. It means that the move of God in the earth realm can only be brought about through you. Better still, wherever you go, God goes. When you show up in a place, God shows up. Hallelujah! Listen! You are more than a man. The Bible declares that your body is the temple of the Holy Ghost (1 Corinthians 6:19). This temple represents a "God Zone" everywhere it goes. This means that your presence in a place is a God Zone in that place. Therefore, nothing that is anti-Christ is permitted to operate when there is a God Zone. In 2 Corinthians 3:17 (NIV), the scriptures declare that "...the Lord is the Spirit, and where the Spirit of the Lord is, there is freedom". In other words, the presence of the Spirit in any place is an automatic God Zone.

Not only is your life void of worry, it also represents a God Zone. Hence, your presence in a place should usher in a worry-free zone. Sadly, many of God's people are not even aware that worrying is anti-Christ, not to mention bring a worry-free zone to others. Many Christians worry about their kids, spouse, bills, job, house, and even about the weather. It appears they worry about everything, what a life! That's not what Jesus died for. In John 10:10 (NLT) Jesus said, "...My purpose is to give them a rich and satisfying life," and He has. So why are so many not living a rich and satisfying life? It is simply because of their unbelief. It is likely that the word of God has not yet been unveiled to their spirits and this is the reason for the teaching of the word of God and praying for the saints. Apostle Paul by the Spirit prayed for the Ephesians saints and in his prayer, he prayed, "Open the eyes of their hearts, and let the light of Your truth flood in...." Ephesians 1:18 (VOICE)

He also prayed that the saints grasp the immensity of this glorious way of life- the God Life. Do you realize that your presence in a place is God's weapon against fear, anxiety and everything that does not accord to the Word of God? We read earlier in 2 Corinthians 3:17 that "...the Lord is the Spirit, and where the Spirit of the Lord is, there is freedom." Therefore, when you show up, God shows up in you and a God zone is created, causing worry to automatically lose its ability to thrive.

To activate this God Zone, you must align your spirit with the Word. For example, in Philippians 4:6 (VOICE) the scriptures declare, "Don't be anxious about things; instead, pray..." your response should always be a YES! I refuse to be anxious. Praise God! Think about it, if you are still anxious about things and people, how can you usher in the worry-free zone to others? One thing you must understand is that, whenever the enemy goes after an individual, he (enemy) is really after everything and everyone that is in that person's circle of influence. In other words, what the enemy is really after is the God Zone that limits his ability to carry out his enterprise.

Brothers and sisters, I declare to you a mystery; YOU ARE SATAN'S LIMITATION IN THE EARTH, for the Bible declares, "For the secret power of lawlessness is already at work; but the one who now holds it back will continue to do so till he is taken out of the way." (2 Thessalonians 2:7 NIV) This limitation is the presence of the Holy Spirit in you.

When you feel overwhelmed by adverse circumstances, relax! And declare that you already have the victory over it. As you do so, your God zone is maintained and the influence is extended to your family, co-workers, friends and neighbors.

Faith-Filled Confession:
I refuse to complain, worry, or fear another day of my life. I have a beautiful life and an exciting life because I am born again with the life and nature of God. Therefore, I refuse to be anxious, depressed, or afraid. I am a victor over hell, Satan, and death. I am different. I know who I am. Everything about me has been brought to perfection by the Holy Ghost and all things work together for my good. In Jesus' Name.

PEACE FROM WITHIN

"Peace I leave with you; My peace I give you. I do not give to you as the world gives. Do not let your hearts be troubled and do not be afraid." (John 14:27 NIV)

No Christians should be engaged in battles that

Jesus already won on their behalf. If after all that He did for us, how can we continue to engage the same adversary whom He overwhelmingly defeated? If we are, then something is wrong with our theology. Such practice is proof that we are operating outside of the Word.

For example, when it comes to peace, you were given peace at salvation. Yet, so many Christians live lives that are characterized by war and commotion; they turn to various vices, all to gain peace. But then Jesus said, "I am leaving you with a gift—peace of mind...." (John 14:27 NLT) This means that you have all that you require to live a peaceful life. The day you got saved, the peace of God came into you; so, you no longer have to pray for peace. Jesus has become your peace. Isaiah 9:6 called Him the Prince of Peace. Jesus said, "And be sure of this: I am with you always, even to the end of the age." (Matthew 28:20 NLT) If this is true, why would any Christian confess that they lack peace in their life or home? Many of us do not realize this, but when your confession contradicts the person and ministry of Jesus, you reject the power and ministry of Jesus in your life. Consequently, you cannot expect to see the manifestation or reality of what He has done in your life.

Child of God, you have peace of mind. Your life is peaceful and beautiful. The peace that you have in Christ is not external; it is not connected to anything or anyone. Jesus said, "Peace I leave with you; my peace I give you. I do not give to you as the world gives. Do not let your hearts be troubled and do not be afraid." (John 14:27 NIV) Why did Jesus distinguish between the peace which He gives and the one which the world gives? He did so because He did not want us to confuse material peace with divine peace. For example, one could say, "I will have peace when I pay my bills." But such peace is material and of the world and has no connection to divine peace which is from God. Such an outlook will rob any Christian from enjoying the true peace that is in Jesus

Christ. Too many have settled for worldly peace without realizing it. They connect their peace to their marriage, job, children, bank accounts and so on. If, as a Christian, your peace is dependent on favorable conditions in your marriage, job, or anything else other than the person of Jesus, you are short-changing yourself and may never experience true peace.

The presence of Jesus in you is peace, and this peace does not bow to anything that is contrary to Christ and His finished work. When Jesus spoke about peace, He wasn't referring to the absence of adverse circumstances. When He spoke of peace, He was dealing with power - a state of victory over the elements of this world. He said to His disciples in John 16:33 (AMPC), "I have told you these things, so that in Me you may have [perfect] peace *and confidence.* In the world you have tribulation *and trials and distress and frustration*; but be of good cheer [take courage; be confident, certain, undaunted]! For I have overcome the world. [I have deprived it of power to harm you and have conquered it for you.]" In other words, the difficulties that you may encounter are not to your detriment because Jesus already deprived them of power to harm you and have conquered them for you. On the other hand, each challenge is conditioned to pull you to your next level. With each situation you will find revelation; and with revelation, you will find promotion.

Have no fear whatsoever. Refuse to be troubled by any bad news. Just do what Jesus did: speak peace! And after you have spoken peace, let your mind stay on the Word. The peace of God in you is the power over adverse circumstances. Declare it every time!

Faith-Filled Confession:
I am not afraid of the terror by night or the arrow that flies by day, or the pestilence that stalks in the darkness, or the plague that destroys at midday. A thousand may fall at my side, ten thousand at my right hand, but it will not come near me. For the Lord is my refuge and my fortress. In Him alone is my trust. He is my peace.

A PEACEMAKER

"So then, let us aim for harmony in the church and try to build each other up." (Romans 14:19 NLT)

I am yet to see someone who is divisive, full of complaints, and self-centered thrive in God's grace; they never do. To people like this, others are usually the problem. Saints, you must shut down anyone or any situation that encourages division. Period! For the sake of your marriage, children, and wellbeing deal wisely with those who are divisive, full of complaints and self-centered, and if that doesn't work, RUN! If you expect the anointing to rest on you and your home, you should not tolerate any form of schism or tolerate those who subtly undercut others. A divisiveness environment is an environment where God's Spirit will not function. This is the reason why many can't linger in communion with the Holy Ghost. We know that God can do all things, but He will not command His anointing to manifest in a divisiveness environment. Psalm 133:1-3 (NLT) declares; "How wonderful and pleasant it is when brothers live together in harmony! For harmony is as precious as the anointing oil that was poured over Aaron's head, that ran down his beard and onto the border of his robe. Harmony is as refreshing as the dew from Mount Hermon that falls on the mountains of Zion. And there the Lord has pronounced His blessing, even life everlasting."

I want you to notice the expression "...And there the Lord has pronounced His blessing, even life everlasting." The pronouncement of the blessing is rooted in harmony; when you are in-sync with the Word and at peace with others. In 2 Corinthians 2:11 (ESV) when the scripture declares that "We would not be outwitted by Satan; for we are not ignorant of his designs," the subject matter there was forgiveness. As a child of God, some things are inconsistent with the nature of God in you. When it comes to championing peace, you shouldn't wait for anyone to encourage you. It is your lifestyle as a child of God. It doesn't matter how much you know, if your knowledge of the Word does not stir you to be at peace with others, it means that your knowledge of the Word is baseless. Listen; God is not as concerned about what others do to you or say about you, as He is about how you respond to what may have been said or done to you. If you are thinking of an occasion to walk in darkness as a child of God, sorry there isn't one.

If you desire to have the plan of God for your life fulfilled, you should not tolerate anyone around you who speaks ill of others; especially ministers of the gospel. Make your stand very clear to them. It's better to hurt their feelings at that moment to save yourself and that person in the long run. Jesus said in Matthew 18:15 (NIV) "If your brother or sister sins, go and point out their fault, just between the two of you. If they listen to you, you have won them over. But if they will not listen, take one or two others along, so that 'every matter may be established by the testimony of two or three witnesses.' If they still refuse to listen, tell it to the church; and if they refuse to listen even to the church, treat them as you would a pagan or a tax collector."

Saints, certain things are too high for us. It is not our responsibility to judge or score ministers on how well they are doing. You may not have been taught this, but whenever a man or woman speaks ill of God's anointed, they are speaking by an evil spirit whose only aim is to destroy the one speaking ill of the minister and to undercut the authority of the man or a woman of God. Proverbs 6:16-19 says that there are six things that the Lord hates: yea, the seventh one is an abomination unto Him which is a person that sows' discord among brethren. Whenever someone speaks ill of others to you, the aim of the devil is to get you to partake of something that can cause the anointing to cease its operation in your life. However, be wise! Tell them to take their grievances to the person with whom they have the issue because that's the way to resolve conflict and to shut the devil out of your life.

Be at peace my fellow saint; the Lord wants to use you for His glory. Don't be neutral or silent when someone is speaking ill of another person. And if you have spoken ill of others, repent and ask God to forgive you. Be wise and be a peacemaker because there is a flow of the anointing that ought to be evident in your life today. And if others have treated you badly, forgive them. Pray that God will increase the knowledge of His will in them. Don't pray for their misery or downfall, No! Don't do that. See them with the eyes of love only.

Faith-Filled Confession:
I speak wholesome words; words that are full of grace. I am known by love and I give no room for division. If anyone has wronged me, I forgive them from my spirit. I refuse to harbor unforgiveness or bitterness. I am a love being; the love of God has been shed abroad in my heart by the Holy Ghost. I only have love to give.

p r a i s e

I am going to praise God with joy unspeakable
because I know that God never fails and His Word in me
will not fail either

THE POWER OF PRAISE (Pt. I)

"Let the people praise thee, O God; let all the people praise thee. Then shall the earth yield her increase; and God, even our own God, shall bless us." (Psalm 67:5-6 KJV)

Praise is a great weapon of choice when it comes to silencing hell's assault on your destiny. You cannot rise above your level of praise; your praise defines God's supernatural influence through you; by your praise, you can determine how much of God's grace will be made manifest in your life. The Lord is calling us unto exceeding praise, by which we will ascend in the marketplace of life. This kind of praise is not based on what God has done; it transcends the material manifestations of the wonders of His grace. Anyone can praise God when they get healed of cancer, even unsaved people do that. What God is calling for, is an exceeding, unrestricted, pure praise; one that comes from a place of intimacy and revelation.

Shadrach, Meshach, and Abednego engaged in this kind of praise when they were made to choose between bowing down to an idol god and being thrown into the fiery furnace to face death. In the face of death, they declared, "...O Nebuchadnezzar, we are not careful to answer thee in this matter. If that's the case, our God whom we serve is able to deliver us from the burning fiery furnace, and He will deliver us out of thine hand, O king. But if not, be it known unto thee, O king, that we will not serve thy gods, nor worship the golden image which thou hast set up." (Daniel 3:16-18 KJV) Their worship transcended what God had done or what God was going to do. They were ready to do what was right even if it meant facing the consequence of death. That's the kind of praise that Jesus offered to His Father and that is the kind of praise that you have been anointed to give.

Exceeding praise is that praise that will not bow to situations or circumstances. It is an audacious expression of one's faith. It is the consciousness that you have all that you need in Christ Jesus. It's the consciousness of worship and deep reverence for the Word. It is the kind of praise that Jesus spoke about in John 4:23 (NIV) when He said to the woman at the well, "Yet a time is coming and has now come when the true worshipers will worship the Father in the Spirit and in truth, for they are the kind of worshipers the Father seeks."

Child of God, I believe the time is now. And you are that true worshipper that Jesus spoke about. Hence, you must seek to know the Father beyond what He does, and seek to know Him for who He is; only then can you truly offer Him exceeding praise. Besides, He saved you for just that: to have a relationship with you that isn't based on what He has done for you or what you can get from Him. His desire has always been to have a Father-son/daughter relationship with you. Let that be your desire as well – to have a solid relationship with your Heavenly Father who loves you more than you could ever know or imagine.

Faith-Filled Confession:
I will extol You, my God, O King; I will bless Your name forever and ever. Every day I will bless You, and I will praise Your name forever and ever. Great is the Lord, and greatly to be praised. His greatness is unsearchable. One generation shall praise Your works to another, and shall declare Your mighty acts. I will meditate on the glorious splendor of Your majesty, and on Your wondrous works forever. Men shall speak of the might of Your awesome acts, and I will declare Your greatness forever. (Psalm 145:1-6 NKJV)

THE POWER OF PRAISE (Pt. II)

"I will bless the Lord at all times; His praise shall continually be in my mouth." (Psalm 34:1 NKJV)

Praise is a weapon that can reverse the irreversible. It can destroy cancer, restore relationships, unstop deaf ears, change death sentences, and the list goes on. It is a very potent weapon, especially when it's done by revelation. Many engage in what they call "praise and worship", yet the manifestation of the glory that ought to follow true praise is absent in their lives. And this is primarily because people praise God, but they do it without revelation. Throughout the scriptures, we find the unstoppable power of praise in demonstration; nations were literally brought to their knees when praise activated the Shekinah glory. I'll say it this way; if a fiery furnace of fire could not bring the three Hebrews boys to their knees, I am telling you right now that no situation or condition can change what Jesus has already done for you. No cancer, sickness, lack or hell can reverse the divine order over your life. You will live and not die until you fulfill God's will for your life.

Take stock of what God has done in your life and in the lives of those around you. Meditate on His goodness until praise erupts in your soul. Focus only on the greatness of the name of Jesus Christ and recall the mercies of God over your life. Only then can you experience the true meaning of praise. And with such praise, anything is possible! Even death sentences can be reversed. Hezekiah did just that. By pledging praise to God, he was able to reverse a death sentence that was issued by God Himself. In 2 Kings 20, God sent word through His prophet, Isaiah, to tell Hezekiah that he was going to die. Rather than accept that death sentence, Hezekiah turned his face to the wall and petitioned God. The Bible says, "Before Isaiah had left the middle court, the Word of the Lord came to him: "Go back and tell Hezekiah, the ruler of my people, 'This is what the Lord, the God of your father David, says: I have heard your prayer and seen your tears; I will heal you. I will add fifteen years to your life. And I will deliver you and this city from the hand of the king of Assyria. I will defend this city for my sake, and for the sake of my servant David." (2 Kings 20:4-6 NIV)

Saints, no condition cannot be turned around by true praise to God. You may have received a terrible report, but if you would learn to look away from that report and focus your attention on the power of God, and praise Him, there will be a change. Now, I see why there were so many miracles in David's life. He said, "I will bless the Lord at all times; His praise shall continually be in my mouth." (Psalm 34:1 NKJV) And the more he praised God, the more miracles he experienced. And I believe the same will be your portion. Be filled with praise, no matter what happens. There is power in praising God.

Faith-Filled Confession:
God—You're my God! I can't get enough of You! I've worked up such hunger and thirst for God, traveling across dry and weary deserts. So here I am in the place of worship, eyes open, drinking in Your strength and glory. In your generous love, I am really living at last! My lips brim praises like fountains. I bless You every time I take a breath; my arms wave like banners of praise to You. (Psalm 63:1-4 MSG)

PRAISE WITH UNDERSTANDING

"I will bless the LORD at all times; His praise shall continually be in my mouth." (Psalm 34:1 NKJV)

God does not want us to do things just because others are doing it. His desire is for our words and actions to come from a place of revelation; from a personal encounter with Him. For only then can it be by faith. Hebrews 11:6 (BLB) says, "without faith, it is impossible to please Him." If your desire is to please God, then your manner of life must be rooted in the Word of God; this includes your praise to God. I have seen people get into a "praise dance"; shout, and run simply because they saw others doing it. There is nothing wrong with being inspired by others to run and dance, but if you do, make sure that it is coming from a place of your personal encounter or testimony of God. On the other hand, if you do all of that simply because you saw others do it, it would be wrong and fruitless. Jesus calls it vain worship and praise. I have witnessed occasions where praise dancing became an act of who can dance better. Jesus said in Mark 7:6-7 (NIV), "...These people honor me with their lips, but their hearts are far from me. They worship me in vain; their teachings are merely human rules." In other words, they say the right words, and move like they are in rhythm with the Spirit, but their hearts are not in agreement with their words and actions. Jesus said in Mark 7:7, "they worship Me in vain." The Greek word that's translated "vain" in this verse is *matēn. Matēn* means *fruitlessly.* They do so out of tradition and custom; with no deep conviction or revelation.

Ask yourself this question: "Is my praise fruitless or done out of revelation?" You really don't have to answer this question because your quality of life will reveal the root of your praise to God. Truth be told, if your praise is rooted in revelation, your life would be full of joy and testimonies. But if testimonies and miracles are scarce in your life, you need to re-examine your attitude to praise and ask God to reveal Himself to you. When David said "I will bless the Lord at all times..." it was more than mere confessing. It was a quality decision he made to bless the Lord at all times; one that came from a place of revelation and encounter with God. To David, the condition of his surroundings was not going to influence His praise to God. I am reminded of what the prophet said in Habakkuk 3:17-18. He said, "Though the fig tree should not blossom and there be no fruit on the vines, though the yield of the olive should fail and the fields produce no food, though the flock should be cut off from the fold and there be no cattle in the stalls, yet I will rejoice in the Lord, I will joy in the God of my salvation." (NASB) Listen, ordinary people don't talk like this; it takes someone who has lost touch with earthly realities to declare, "I will rejoice in the Lord, I will joy in the God of my salvation" in the midst of the worst recession.

What am I saying to you? Don't be a copycat. If you must run, dance, and jump like you don't care, let it be from a place of revelation. Let your mind be full of the wonder of His grace. As you praise today, recall all that He has done in your life. Jeremiah 51:50 (KJV) says "Ye that have escaped the sword, go away, stand not still: remember the Lord afar off, and let Jerusalem come into your mind." As you praise God, let His eternal Word burn on your lips; let His goodness and faithfulness towards you come to your mind.

Faith-Filled Confession:
I thank You Father that the righteous cannot be forsaken, neither does his seed beg for bread. I thank You that every need is supplied in Christ Jesus and that I have been made a victor eternally. I bring into compliance every contrary situation and circumstance lurking around my life today. I declare that I am fruitful and productive in all areas of my life. For as Jesus is in Heaven, so am I on the earth; triumphant, healthy, and strong. Hallelujah!

LET THE PRAISE BEGIN

"And the LORD said unto Joshua, "This day will I begin to magnify thee in the sight of all Israel, that they may know that, as I was with Moses, so I will be with thee." (Joshua 3:7 KJV)

While ministering at a church some time ago, I heard a song that has echoed in my spirit for days. The chorus of the song says, "You are great, you are great, you are great, and everything written about you is great." Wow! Isn't that the truth? Everything written about our God from Genesis to Revelation is beyond great. Praise God! A few days after, this same song came up in my spirit, but this time, the Spirit of God was singing it over me. Initially, I felt uneasy; I felt this was a song for God alone. But He kept singing it over me, and the Lord said to me, "Everything I have written about you is great. Tell me one thing that I have done or said about you that isn't great." By this time, I was speechless because everything He has done and said has been beyond great. Then He said, "Do you see why it's no longer permissible for you to walk around weak and ordinary? I have said that I will begin to magnify you in the sight of all men that they may know that, as I was with Moses, Joshua, Elijah, Paul, Peter, and the prophets and apostles of old, so I AM with you." Then He continued to sing over and over, saying, "I have given you My greatness and everything that man will see and say concerning you from this day will be greatness. For in this season, I have caused Heaven to touch the earth specifically for you." Hallelujah!

Saints, these words were not directed at me alone; they were for you as well if you would believe. The Lord says, "I am doing this for all my children right now. Tell them to open their eyes and see that I AM DOING A NEW THING and that the victory song over them is GREATNESS, HONOR, AND PRAISE. Tell them to see nothing but greatness in everything. The days of not knowing what to do are over, for the anointing has been sent forth with greater intensity to dissolve every element of doubt and put to end every form of harassment."

Child of God, it's time to plug into this anointing. Put these words before your eyes; seed your subconscious with them. Declare them over yourself day and night. Remember that these words are eternally settled in Heaven. It's up to you to make it your reality by believing in it. Say like Mary, "It's established unto me as it has been spoken by God." Declare that it is time for uncommon favor and honor.

I decree over you right now: you are unstoppable! Anyone who will attempt to stand in your way for the sole purpose of causing you to stumble on these prophetic words will be put to shame. They will watch your elevation to greatness. In Jesus' name! It's your time to be HONORED, so praise God!

Faith-Filled Confession:
I am anointed and appointed by the Holy Ghost to display glory, honor and power. Everywhere I go, I expect nothing short of greatness and honor by the Holy Ghost. Therefore, I declare favor, greatness and honor follows me today. I see men and women coming from all over the world to favor and honor me. In Jesus' name! Amen!

UNRESTRICTED PRAISE

"I will become even more undignified than this, and I will be humiliated in my own eyes. But by these slave girls you spoke of, I will be held in honor." (2 Samuel 6:22 NIV)

Praising God without a revelation of His person is like trying to drive a car without wheels. You can engage in the jamboree of praise and still not be effective in praise. Singing, shouting, and jumping does not always mean that one is praising God. If you have ever attended a worldly concert, you would attest to the fact that they also have singing, shouting, and dancing. What makes your singing, shouting, and dancing different from theirs is your revelation of the one to whom you are singing, shouting and dancing. God has no interest in religion. He doesn't want you to do anything for the sake of doing. He is a God of purpose and everything He does is according to His Word; if He is going to receive anything from us, then it must be in accordance with His Word. If we are going to engage in meaningful and effective praise, then we must praise with the Word in our spirit. Our singing and gesticulation must be inspired by our revelation of who He is to us.

You cannot praise God effectively based on someone else's revelation or encounter. The praise that provokes the power of God on your behalf is that praise that comes from your spirit; that praise that comes from your personal encounter with Him. When you study in 2 Samuel 6, the Bible tells us of how Michal, David's wife, despised David in her heart because of how he danced and rejoiced before the Lord. David's undignified praise to God before his subjects was embarrassing to her. She said, "How the king of Israel has distinguished himself today, going around half-naked in full view of the slave girls of his servants as any vulgar fellow would!" (2 Samuel 6:20 NIV) She did not have David's revelation of praise, and she obviously had not had David's kind of encounters with God. If she had, I dare say that she would have done even more. Sometimes, we see people crying, shouting, running around the church, seeds, and committing to partnership in the house of God; there is a reason why they do such things. They really don't have to explain it to anybody. I know that in some quarters, expressing yourself that way is prohibited. But I say, if you feel like you have to shout, then SHOUT! If there is a pull in your spirit to run, I say run! But all things must be done in an orderly fashion. No one should feel hindered from praising God the way they deem fit. To David, seeing the ark of God return to the City of David was worth praising and rejoicing about, even if it meant him becoming undignified.

I love David's response to his wife in 2 Samuel 6:21,22 (NIV), "It was before the Lord, who chose me rather than your father or anyone from his house when he appointed me ruler over the Lord's people Israel—I will celebrate before the Lord. I will become even more undignified than this, and I will be humiliated in my own eyes. But by these slave girls you spoke of, I will be held in honor." In other words, David lost consciousness of his kingship because he was standing before the true King. He knew that his audience was not men but God and that made the difference. He was conscious of only one person and that person was God Almighty. As he recalled all that the ark represented in his kingdom and in his life, he could not help but let go of his pride and status.

I want to encourage you, whether privately or publicly, let Jesus and His finished work stay on your mind as you praise God. Bring to remembrance all that the name of Jesus represents in your life and let that inspire you to praise God the way that the Spirit pulls you to do. Papa God deserves an undignified praise from you.

Faith-Filled Confession:
Be magnified O Lord! You are the Almighty God; the maker of all things. Before time began, you were. Before Heaven was created, you existed. Nothing catches You by surprise. You are Alpha and Omega. Excellent God! Every praise belongs to You! You live forever! You reign forever! My Rock and my Salvation, I will praise You for all eternity.

I WILL REJOICE NO MATTER WHAT

"I will be glad and rejoice in You; I will sing the praises of Your name, O Most High." (Psalm 9:2 NIV)

Each day, we are presented with situations that could make us complain, and some of these situations provide legitimate grounds for complaining if evaluated from a logical perspective. However, from the viewpoint of the kingdom of God, there is no credible reason for complaining. The scripture says, "Do all things without grumbling or disputing." (Philippians 2:14 ESV) Notice that it said "all things" not some things. Child of God, there is no glory in complaining. It only attracts and creates the right environment for darkness to thrive. I am yet to see a man that complained through life that was able to achieve anything that could be considered to be praiseworthy. For the most part, they blame others for their predicaments, which in turn, sets in motion an unending circle of defeat and hopelessness. And sadly, many feel hopeless over the very thing that God has called them to dominate.

Jesus was never one to complain or blame others for the challenges that He faced. Unlike John the Baptist, who at one point, blamed Jesus for not coming to his rescue while he was in jail. John sent his disciples to ask Jesus in Matthew 11:3 (NIV), "Are you the one who is to come, or should we expect someone else?" In other words, John was saying to Jesus, "Why aren't You doing something about my situation?" People can complain all they want and blame others for why they are where they are, but at the end of the day, no one is responsible for your situation, not even God can be blamed. Jesus' response to John the Baptist made it clear that He was not responsible for John's predicament. Because of everyone born of a woman until this time, John the Baptist was considered to be the greatest. He carried something that no one before him ever carried and so if he wanted to get out of that jail, he had the power to do so. He had what was necessary to change his situation.

So, do not take the bait of complaining; rather, rejoice! Even when you think you have a legitimate reason to complain, do not complain! Rejoice instead! Offer praise and thanksgiving to God, for that is the way to rise above it all. Jesus is our great example. When He was rejected by those who should have been His biggest fans, He didn't get bitter and hurl insults on them. He didn't call them "destiny killers" like some of us do today. He was amazed at their unbelief, but rather than act out of character, He continued to teach from village to village. So, no matter what you may face, "Always be full of joy in the Lord. I say it again—rejoice!" (Philippians 4:4 NLT)

Faith-Filled Confession:
I have been raised together with Christ and made to sit together with Christ in Heavenly places; far above sickness, lack, pain and every principality of darkness. I am one with my Father. I am born of His Spirit. I know who I am and I am alive to who I am in Christ Jesus. Hallelujah!

BE ON THE OFFENSIVE WITH PRAISE

"But the one who rules in heaven laughs. The Lord scoffs at them." (Psalm 2:4 NLT)

The best response to any form of distraction is to be joyful with praise. We see this with God. In Psalm 2:1-4, the scripture says, "Why are the nations so angry? Why do they waste their time with futile plans? The kings of the earth prepare for battle; the rulers plot together against the Lord and against His anointed one. 'Let us break their chains,' they cry, 'and free ourselves from slavery to God.' But the one who rules in heaven laughs. The Lord scoffs at them." (NLT) And the scripture tells us to be imitators of God (Ephesians 5:1). In every situation, we ought to laugh and rejoice with unspeakable joy. Truth be told, we are not in any way disadvantaged; come what may, we are eternal victors in Christ, over the world, hell, and every demon of darkness. Some may call us nonchalant because we refuse to be disturbed by things happening around us. Some may go as far as calling us arrogant, but we are not. We are simply confident about the ministry of the Holy Spirit in our lives. There is a knowing on the inside of us that "Greater is He who is in us, than whatever may be out there in the world." We just know that failure is not an option. Think of it this way: God is not moved by circumstances and neither should we. I know some folks will say, "But Pastor, we are not God." But you are a child of God, right? Besides, the Bible says in 1 Corinthians 6:17, "But he that is joined unto the Lord is one spirit." (KJV) This means that whatever happens to you happens to Him. If He is not moved, then I am not moved. Praise God!

Make up your mind to not get distracted from God's course for your life. Stand unshakable against every element of distraction because victory is already yours. There is a path of prosperity, joy, miracles, and unstoppable increase and expansion that God has set before you. Hebrews 12:2 tells us what Jesus did when distractions came to derail Him from the course of life that Papa God had set before Him. The Bible says "...who for the joy that was set before Him endured the cross, despising the shame, and is seated at the right hand of the throne of God." (ESV) Let nothing derail you from it. No matter what has happened, the victory is in your spirit. Speak it out loud. Glory!

1 Peter 1:8 (GWT) says "Although you have never seen Christ, you love Him. You don't see Him now, but you believe in Him. You are extremely happy with joy and praise that can hardly be expressed in words." This same faith that is demonstrated concerning the person of Jesus is what God expects you to display over every distraction. In other words, rejoice in every situation; rejoice even when your desired result has not yet manifested. I am going to praise God with joy unspeakable because I know that God never fails and His Word in me will not fail as well. Say like David, "I will bless the Lord at all times; His praise shall continually be in my mouth." (Psalm 34:1 NKJV)

Faith-Filled Confession:
My faith is unwavering; my trust is in God alone. I believe the Word of God with my whole being. And I know that He that has begun a good work in me will surely bring it to completion. I rejoice in Jesus! Amen.

REJOICING IS MY WAY OF LIVING

"It is written: "I believed; therefore, I have spoken." Since we have that same spirit of faith, we also believe and therefore speak" (2 Corinthians 4:13 NIV)

There is so much for us to rejoice over if only we will make the decision to see life through the prism of the Word. I do understand that sometimes we are faced with challenging situations. But, regardless of the situation, rejoice! Because when it comes to rejoicing, it has nothing to do with how you feel or what challenges you face. Rejoicing ought to be your way of life.

As Christians, our lives ought to be guided by the Word of God. When we rejoice in the face of adversity, it may not make any sense to those in the flesh, but we do so with an understanding of the Word. We rejoice because adverse circumstances are opportunities to put our faith to work. Think about it; how else would the people of the world know that Jesus is the same yesterday, today and forever, if we are never presented with opportunities to display the miraculous working power of God?

Child of God, you are not of them that flee in the face of adversity. You do not retreat! You are born again! Greater is He that is in you than he that is in the world. You belong to the family of victors headed by Jesus. Your spiritual progenitors called adversity bread and spoke boldly in the Lord. They casted out devils, healed the sick and raised the dead. Hebrews 11:33–34 (AMPC) gives a description of how they "...subdued kingdoms, administered justice, obtained promised blessings, closed the mouths of lions, extinguished the power of raging fire, escaped the devouring of the sword, out of frailty and weakness won strength and became stalwart, even mighty and resistless in battle, routing alien hosts." You must understand that the person that you see each time you look in the mirror is not a weakling or a failure. You are a victor! Inside you lies the power that created the Heavens and the earth. Don't talk yourself away from any opportunity to move to a higher level. Don't allow the testimony of others about any given situation change the truth that you already have the victory.

Live independent of circumstances and let the Word be your driving force. If the Word says, "consider it pure joy...whenever you face trials of many kinds" (James 1:2 NIV), then count it all joy! Don't ask "how can I?" Rejoice, because you can! You are more than a conqueror! Remember that God will never ask you to do anything that He has not equipped you to do. Think of it this way; picture a five-year-old demanding a wrestling contest from a professional boxer. Not only is this laughable, but it's also not worth taking seriously. This ought to be your mindset as you go out today. Regardless of the challenge out there, it is no match for the firepower of the Holy Ghost that's on the inside of you.

Go about your day with a smile on your face. Laugh and rejoice like one who has just won the lottery. Get excited about your life! There is more to you than meets the eye. At the end of the day, what really matters is the reign of Christ through you. Make it count!

Faith-Filled Confession:
I rejoice in the Lord; I rejoice at His Word. The joy of the Lord is my strength. Greater is He that is in me than he that is in the world. I am victorious in Christ; triumphant on every count; more than a conqueror; advancing by the power of the Holy Ghost. I have no sad or down days. My life is from glory to glory; unstoppable by any human or demonic force. Hallelujah!

p r a y e r

Praying with joy would mean praying with confident
assurance that whatever God says is done

EXERCISE YOURSELF IN PRAYER

"And He spake a parable unto them to this end, that men ought always to pray, and not to faint." (Luke 18:1 KJV)

I am yet to see a Christian that does not love prayer. We all love prayer, but what we really love about prayer is the effect of it. We all know that prayer can move mountains, but then when we call for prayer, in most cases, only very few respond to pray. Jesus said, "... men ought always to pray, and not to faint." (Luke 18:1 KJV) Prayer is a necessity in exercising the God-life. It is the spinal cord of your relationship with your Heavenly Father. Imagine being in a relationship with someone with whom you do not communicate, and whenever you do communicate, it's in a bid to get something from them. This is what many have reduced prayer to. The only time they pray is when they want God to do something; not knowing that such attitude is responsible for lack of answers to their prayers. Saints, prayer was never designed to get God to do anything about any situation. It is the effect of prayer or fellowship with Him that gets things going in the right direction.

God does not want to hear from you only when you see trouble coming, and when it's gone, you are nowhere to be found. His will is that you remain in a place of constant renewal by the Holy Ghost. This is what constant fellowship in prayer does. It keeps you tuned up, builds you up, and empowers you to walk in the Spirit (Galatians 5:16).

When it comes to prayer, the emphasis is on praying the Word and not simply talking, because anybody can just talk. The key to an effective and consistent prayer life that tones you up spiritually is the Word. In Hosea 14:2 (NKJV), the Spirit of God said through the prophet, "Take words with you..." He was pretty much saying, "Bring the divine Word of God that is revealed to your spirit with you." There is nothing that delights the Father's heart and stirs or tunes you up for victory and excellence like speaking forth the Word in fellowship with Him. Remember that Papa God is a faith God, which means that everything He does is according to His

Word. He doesn't see anything outside of His Word. His Word is His limit and His Word is limitless! Praise God! Hallelujah!

Imagine starting your day with a prayer like this: "Father, in the name of the Lord Jesus, I thank You that I have divine ability at work in me. I do not make haste; I am conscious of my divinity today. I function with this consciousness that I have love, joy, peace, patience, kindness, goodness, faithfulness, gentleness, self-control. I live an excellent life that is full of the demonstration of the Spirit. Hallelujah!" Such a prayer will tune your spirit up for victory and prosperity in no time. Contrast that with starting your day with a prayer like this: "O Lord, give me peace, joy and help me because my life is full of ups and downs." I can assure you that the latter prayer would not only tune down your spirit; it will also set you on a course of faithlessness and unbelief because it's not according to His Word.

Brothers and sisters, let's get into the Word today with excitement, knowing that no word from God is void of power (Luke 1:37 ASV). And let's begin the most glorious part of our day - our communion with the Holy Spirit.

Faith-Filled Confession:
Father, in the name of the Lord Jesus, I thank You that I have divine ability at work in me. I function with the consciousness that I have love, joy, peace, patience, kindness, goodness, faithfulness, gentleness, and self-control. I live an excellent life; full of the demonstration of the Spirit. And I bless my world today with the presence of God. Hallelujah!

LOOK INWARDS WHEN YOU PRAY

"He who did not spare His own Son but gave Him up for us all, how will He not also, along with Him, freely give us all things?" (Romans 8:32 BSB)

A beggarly mindset in the place of prayer is a function of ignorance of God's Word. As a child of God, there is nothing that you require in this world that your Heavenly Father has not already delivered to you. So, you do not have to drool all over the place with the hope that God answers you. Remember that you are in this world on the account of Jesus; you are here as a representative of the Kingdom of Heaven. Jesus said, "... as the Father has sent Me, even so I am sending you." (John 20:21 ESV) And because you are sent, all that you require to function as a God-kind has already been made available to you. Paul the Apostle once asked a question, "Whoever goes to war at his own expense?" (1 Corinthians 9:7 NKJV) The answer is emphatically NO ONE!

Understand that the Christian is not a beggar; so, let no one deceive you. Have you noticed that those whose prayers are characterized by "give me, give me Lord" appear to not be getting anything? It's as though the more they pray "give me, give me Lord", the more the need to pray "give me, give me Lord" arises. Hear me! The Christian is a possessor of all things. The Bible says "...For all things are yours, whether Paul, or Apollos, or Cephas, or the world, or life, or death, or things present, or things to come—all are yours, and you of Christ, and Christ of God." The reason why "give me, give me Lord" does not give anything is because God already gave you all things; He does not have anything more to give you. 2 Peter 1:3 (ESV) declares "His divine power has granted to us all things that pertain to life and godliness, through the knowledge of Him who called us to His own glory and excellence." He has given you all things, even those things which your mind has not yet imagined. Praise God!

One may ask, "So where are these things which God has given me?" They are in your spirit. When the life and nature of God were imparted into your spirit to be born again, heaven came into your spirit. All that heaven is, came on the inside of you in the person of the Holy Spirit. This is the reason Paul declared by the Holy Ghost in Ephesians 3:20 (NKJV), "Now to Him who is able to do exceedingly abundantly above all that we ask or think, according to the power that works in us." The power to do is no longer in heaven; it is in you. This means that your desired miracle is not going to come from Heaven; rather, it's going to come from your spirit. As a young Christian, I was taught that my prayers went up to Heaven and that Heaven was responsible for releasing the supply. I remember one time after I had prayed, I felt like the prayer did not leave my room, so I went outside to avoid any obstacle that was in the way of my prayer reaching heaven. It may sound funny now, but that was all I knew then. No one told me that my prayers didn't need to go through the walls or roof; that the one who hears and answers prayers lives on the inside of me, and that everything that I could ever think of or imagine was already made available to me in Christ Jesus. All I needed to do was to thank God for what He had already done and to enjoy His supply.

Brothers and Sisters, whatever you need is in your spirit. Look inwards; the answer is already on the inside you. Find the provision in the Word and speak it forth in faith. Be bold and let your life produce results, which can only be attributed to the power of God.

Faith-Filled Confession:
I am conscious of the Father in me. He is always with me. He hears me and answers my prayers. He has made all grace abound towards me and has blessed me with all spiritual blessings in Christ Jesus. Now, I make withdrawals by faith. I manifest in the earth realm, that which is already so in the spirit. In Jesus' name, Amen.

PRAY AND RECEIVE

"'And when you pray, do not heap up phrases (multiply words, repeating the same ones over and over) as the Gentiles do, for they think they will be heard for their much speaking." (Matthew 6:7 AMPC)

While listening to the radio, I heard a man on the radio say, "Lord, I just need a same-day delivery answer to my prayer." Then I thought to myself; isn't that what praying in the name of Jesus guarantees according to Mark 11:24 and 1 John 5:14? What then is it with the same-day delivery answer to prayer, when the prayer was said in the name of Jesus? Child of God, no matter how big or common a practice or saying is among Christians, you must endeavor to check it out for yourself.

Many do not receive answers to their prayers because of a wrong understanding of prayer and of how prayer works. This wrong understanding, many times, is the result of false teachings on the subject of prayer; teachings that do not accord to the person of Jesus and His eternal accomplished work. A prayer like, "Father, give me a same-day delivery answer to my prayer" is a demonstration of such false understanding; it has no scriptural basis or bearing. Jesus never instructed us to pray that way. He said, "Therefore I tell you, whatever you ask for in prayer, believe that you have received it, and it will be yours." (Mark 11:24 NIV) In other words, the place of prayer is also the place for receiving and your faith is paramount in your receiving from God. Hebrews 11:6 (NKJV) tells us, "But without faith, it is impossible to please Him, for he who comes to God must believe that He is and that He is a rewarder of those who diligently seek Him." You must also make sure that you are praying according to His will, which is His Word. If you can find it in His Word, then you can release your faith for it. And after you have asked, believe that you have received and then receive!

As you pray, believe that you have received what you have asked the Father for in the name of Jesus and be mindful not to use fillers. Let your prayers be specific. Jesus said in Matthew 6:7 (AMPC),

"And when you pray, do not heap up phrases (multiply words, repeating the same ones over and over) as the Gentiles do, for they think they will be heard for their much speaking." And after you have prayed, let your mannerism reflect your faith. Do not go back to the Lord to ask for a same-day delivery answer because your delivery confirmation is your confidence in God's Word. So, receive instantly in prayer.

Faith-Filled Confession:
By faith, I lay hold of all that is mine in Christ Jesus. I refuse to live a beggarly life. I exercise my rights of sonship and the authority I have in the name of Jesus. I declare that my best days are now. Doors of opportunities are opened to me. Goodness, mercy, favor, health, wealth, joy and peace accompany me every day of my life. In Jesus' name, Amen.

PRAY IN THE AFFIRMATIVE

"If you remain in Me and My words remain in you, ask whatever you wish, and it will be done for you." (John 15:7 NIV)

It was never God's intention that we pray and not get answers to our prayers. Jesus said, "And I will do whatever you ask in My name, so that the Father may be glorified in the Son." (John 14:13 NIV) In other words, it means a lot to God when you receive answers to your prayer. The Father is glorified when your prayers are answered. I know that some see no need for prayer. They believe "what shall be, shall be." Chip Brogden had a great response for such people. He said, "If God will do whatever He wishes, regardless of whether we pray or not, then we do not need to pray at all, and the Lord's instructions on praying for the Kingdom and the Will are superfluous. But the truth is that God waits for a remnant to rise up and to pray in agreement with His Purpose before He does anything – He will do nothing apart from the Church. Apart from Him, we can do nothing; apart from us, He WILL do nothing." Until you realize this simple truth about the way God functions with the Church—the body of Christ—things will happen that could have been averted. You will experience loss when you should have experienced increase.

I want you to understand that life is supernatural, and as a Christian, God has anointed you to determine what happens in your home, community, city, and the nation. And this is why you must meditate on the Word daily. It will show you how to take your place in Christ and bring change to areas that need change. When we fellowship with God's Word, the Holy Spirit brings us into oneness with the reality of the Word. And when this reality gains mastery over our spirits, the abiding victory of Christ is no longer a fairy tale.

When Jesus said, "If ye abide in Me, and My words abide in you, ye shall ask what ye will, and it shall be done unto you" (John 15:7 KJV), He was introducing us to a higher life; a supernatural way of living. If you've ever wondered how Jesus was so full of the miraculous, this was it. It is what I call a "synchronization with the Holy Ghost."

Here is the mystery: God and His Word are one (John 1:1). There is no God without the Word and there is no Word without God. God will never act outside of His Word and the Word is confined to the Father. The Word is unlimited; yet, the only thing that defines what the Father can and cannot do is the Word (Hebrews 6:18). So when you got saved, you came into Christ, and now, you abide in Him (2 Corinthians 5:17; Colossians 3:3). However, it is your responsibility for His Word to abide in you, and this is why He gave you the Holy Spirit. The Holy Spirit helps to uncover the Word to your spirit until the Word is built in you. And when your spirit comes in sync with the Word, your prayer life takes on a new meaning! You will pray with passion because you will always receive and your joy will be in abundance.

Remember, the secret is to pray the Word that the Spirit of God has stirred in your spirit. To pray those Words is to pray the ability of God and to pray the ability of God is to pray in the affirmative. So, the next time you pray, don't pray your senses. Instead, pray the Word from your spirit and be amazed by swift results from God.

You are blessed!

Faith-Filled Confession:
Father, I thank You for Your Word that is built in my spirit. You have given me a life that is not susceptible to defeat, despair, frustration or loss. I give you praise that I have divine health in my body. I experience peace, joy and exceeding prosperity. I declare that I rule over darkness in all its presentations today, in Jesus' name! Amen.

PRAY FOR YOUR CITY AND NATION

"Pray this way for kings and all who are in authority so that we can live peaceful and quiet lives marked by godliness and dignity." (1 Timothy 2:2 NLT)

God has not called us to pray so that we can say

that we prayed. Instead, He has called us to pray because, without our prayers, He cannot intervene in the earth. It is by the prayer of the saints that the will of God is established in the cities and nations of the world. In teaching His disciples to pray, Jesus told them to say: "Your kingdom come, Your will be done, on earth as it is in heaven." (Matthew 6:10 NLT)

God's will for our communities and leaders can only be realized when we pray. 1 Timothy 2:1-3 (NIV) says, "I urge, then, first of all, that petitions, prayers, intercession, and thanksgiving be made for all people— for kings and all those in authority, that we may live peaceful and quiet lives in all godliness and holiness. This is good and pleases God our Savior." We are not called to pray only for those with similar political persuasions, but for ALL in authority, including those with different political views. We must not allow our political affiliations to step in the way of our priestly ministry. Even if you have considered the president to be a foe, you must still pray for the one who sits in the office. In Matthew 5:44 (NKJV), Jesus says, "But I say to you, love your enemies, bless those who curse you, do good to those who hate you, and pray for those who spitefully use you and persecute you."

Remember, as Christians, our affiliation and loyalty is to Christ and Christ ALONE. Our duty is to the different offices occupied by our leaders, and not to individual personalities. So, the occupant of the office should not affect your priestly ministry. Pray regardless of who it is that occupies the office. Pray for your city, pray for your nation, and pray for the nations of the world.

Pray against the agenda of hell, and again, pray for all who are in authority.

God bless you.

Faith-Filled Confession:
I come against every satanic force that is working to create chaos in my nation. I come against every plan of the enemy against our president, state governors, legislative leaders and local government leaders. I declare that the peace of God rules over my city and over my nation. In Jesus' name. Amen

PRAY THE WORD INTO BEING

"Timothy, my child, I entrust to you with this command, which is in accordance with the words of prophecy spoken in the past about you. Use those words as weapons in order to fight well." (1 Timothy 1:18 BSB)

Faith is the mother of all miracles. Behind every fulfilled Word from God is the operation of faith. There is nothing that God has done in the lives of men that didn't require faith. Faith has always and will forever be the catalyst for miracles. Your salvation, which is the greatest miracle of all, came as a result of faith. Jesus said to the woman with the issue of blood, "Your faith has made you whole." (Mark 5:34 KJV) When the disciples were in the midst of a boisterous storm, Jesus asked them, "Where is your faith?" (Luke 8:25 KJV) For the most part, the miracles performed by Jesus were connected to the faith of the recipients of the miracles.

Faith is required to bring to pass the Word that has been spoken over you. Please understand that in God's reality, you already walked into the fullness of the blessing of the Word that was spoken over you. If you fail to work the Word, the Word will do nothing for you. Hebrews 4:2 (KJV) says "For unto us was the gospel preached, as well as unto them: but the word preached did not profit them, not being mixed with faith in them that heard it." In other words, the Word of God that was so full of power became like nothing in their lives simply because they didn't mix the Word with faith. They heard the Word alright, they may have even confessed it, but it accounted for nothing without faith.

The prophet Daniel is a great example of one who was relentless in his faith. He received God's Word but didn't stop there. He didn't fold his hands waiting for something to happen. To Daniel, the Word spoken had to become profitable. And his faith took him to his prayer closet until there was a visible, verifiable, manifestation of the promised Word of God. Did you know that what we have come to know as the Daniel fast was born out of a deep relentless hunger to see the Word come into manifestation? In other words, if

Daniel had prevailed on day forty, we would say today that Daniel's fast is a forty-day fast without pleasant bread. In other words, Daniel didn't have God in a time slot; his attitude was relentless. To Daniel, it didn't matter how long it took, one thing was on his mind; he was not going to relent until the change came to pass and even when it came to pass, he still did not relent.

Saint, let me admonish you by the words of Paul, the Apostle when he admonished his son Timothy: "...I entrust to you this command, which is in accordance with the words of prophecy spoken in the past about you. Use those words as weapons in order to fight well." (1 Timothy 1:18 GNT) In simple terms, Paul was saying to Timothy, "Take the prophetic word that you were given and make war with it in the spirit." In like manner, the Lord is saying to you, "Become steadfast in your confession and intercession; use the prophetic Word for as your inspiration."

Remember that it takes faith for the Word to come to pass.

Faith-Filled Confession:
I walk in dominion by speaking forth God's Word. And as I speak forth God's Word, I see the Word manifest in my life. No Word of God concerning me will return to Him void. The Word of God is productive in me; it does in me exactly what it talks about, in Jesus' name. Amen.

THE PRAYER OF APPROPRIATION

"Therefore I tell you, whatever you ask for in prayer, believe that you have received it, and it will be yours." (Mark 11:24 NIV)

Romans 8:32 (NIV) declares, "He who did not spare His own Son, but gave Him up for us all—how will He not also, along with Him, graciously give us all things?" That is to say, there is nothing that is too good for you. As a child of God, you must realize that the Father delights in you just as He delights in Jesus. And it was the Father's good pleasure to WILL the whole world to you (Romans 8:17, Hebrews 1:2). Jesus said something so profound in John 16:26-27 (NIV). He said, "In that day you will ask in my name. I am not saying that I will ask the Father on your behalf. No, the Father Himself loves you because you have loved me and have believed that I came from God." Brothers and sisters, this statement should destroy the mentality of "I am undeserving" or "I am unworthy," such a mindset has derailed the faith of so many of God's people.

As a child of God, there is nothing that is not already at your disposal (1 Corinthians 3:21-22). All you have to do is to ask in faith. Someone may say, "If all things are mine, why then do I have to ask?" Think about how your bank account works; the money in your account is yours, but there are safety measures in place to protect your money against thieves. The same principle applies in the kingdom (Matthew 6:20). When you pray, you are not begging, you are simply requesting for something that belongs to you. If you pray without the understanding that you are asking for something that already belongs to you, you likely will not receive any answers because such a prayer would not have been done in faith.

There is the prayer of faith and there is the prayer of unbelief. The prayer of faith affirms what has already been done in Christ Jesus. I like to call it the prayer of appropriation; it appropriates whatever grace has already made available to you in Christ Jesus. In Romans 10:6-9 (KJV), the Apostle elucidated this point further when he said, "...Say not in thine heart, who shall ascend into heaven? (that is, to bring Christ down from above:) Or, who shall descend into the deep? (that is, to bring up Christ again from the dead.) But what saith it? The word is nigh thee, even in thy mouth, and in thy heart: that is, the word of faith..." This scripture is simply telling us that there is no amount of prayer and fasting that will change the eternal work of Christ. All we have to do is to align ourselves in the light of what has already been done and affirm it to be so in our lives and this needs to be done with joy.

Praying with joy would mean praying with confident assurance that whatever God says is done. Here is an example: "Father, in the name of the Lord Jesus, I thank You that I have divine ability at work in me. I do not make haste; I am conscious of my divinity today. I function with the consciousness that I have love, joy, peace, patience, kindness, goodness, faithfulness, gentleness, and self-control (Galatians 5:22, 23 NKJV). I live an excellent life that is full of the demonstration of the Spirit. Hallelujah!" Hear me child God, praying and talking like this will tune your spirit up for victory and prosperity in no time. And cause you to appropriate what is yours in Christ Jesus. Remember faith always affirms the WORD and whatever you ask or request in prayer, believe that you have received it, and it will be yours. Praise God!

Faith-Filled Confession:
Father, I thank You in the name of Jesus, that as I pray, I receive, knowing that You have given me all things in Christ Jesus. I see my life through Your Word and when I pray, I pray Your Word with all boldness. And my joy is full because You are not slack on Your Word.

spiritual
discipline

There is no gifting, no amount of accuracy in the prophetic
that can substitute for discipline

BE DISCIPLINED

"Reuben, you are my firstborn, my strength, and the first fruit of my vitality. You excel in rank and excel in power. But you're as undisciplined as a roaring river, so eventually you won't succeed, because you got in your father's bed, defiled it, and then approached my couch." (Genesis 49:3-4 ISV)

If there was anyone of Jacob's children who was suited to excel in life, it was Reuben. Yet, he didn't. And it wasn't because the devil hindered him or because he was faced with an insurmountable circumstance, but Reuben failed in life primarily because he lacked discipline. I have seen many anointed men and women go nowhere in life. They are so gifted, yet they lack the required discipline to execute their assignment. Saint, your God-given ability is no substitute for living a life of discipline. Do not assume that your gift will move you forward if you lack discipline. Someone once said, and I could not have agreed more, that the "anointing without discipline is a death trap." In other words, a fellow who is anointed by God, but lacks self-control is a train wreck going somewhere to wreak havoc.

Many are frustrated by their lack of progress in life, but the reason why they are not experiencing progress is that they lack discipline. They know what God has spoken over their lives, and have at different times, experienced the move of the Spirit. They know the Word and when they talk, they sound "deep." Yet, for some reason, they keep going around in circles; they do not experience the overflow that should accompany such anointing. The reason is simply because of the lack of discipline. There is no gifting; no amount of accuracy in the prophetic that can substitute for discipline. If one lacks discipline, he or she cannot expect to go anywhere in life. Jacob who was anointed and who operated with the prophetic anointing said to Reuben, "Reuben, you're my firstborn, my strength, and the first fruit of my vitality. You excel in rank and excel in power. But you're as undisciplined as a roaring river, so eventually you won't succeed, because you got in your father's bed, defiled it, and then approached my couch."

(Genesis 49:3-4 ISV) Reuben by virtue of his birthright was suited for success. He was equipped for greatness. But his lack of self-control made the anointing that was on him as the first child void. He was reckless with his choices. He was unable to bridle his impulses until he found himself defiling his father's bed.

If you find yourself not making any real headway in life, do not fault anyone or any situation because the problem is not external, the issue is with you. God will not move you to the next level if you lack discipline. Doing things your way will lead you nowhere. Become dependable, reliable and consistent. Note this that every idea is not from God, so stick to those instructions that the Spirit of God has given to you because God will not conform to your way. Be disciplined before it's too late. Get your impulses under the authority of the Word. You are anointed by God, so make it count by living a disciplined life and by sticking to the process.

Faith-Filled Confession:
I give no occasion to the flesh. I yield my mind and my members to the dominion of the Word and the Spirit. I am alert and attentive to the leading of the Holy Spirit. Christ Jesus is glorified in me today and always. Amen.

DISCIPLINE IS LOVE IN ACTION

"For the LORD corrects those he loves, just as a father corrects a child in whom he delights." (Proverbs 3:12 NLT)

Discipleship is a commitment to a lifestyle of discipline. It is subjecting one's desire, opinion, and will to the will of God. Discipleship will cost you your pride and flesh, which you don't need anyway because they are destiny killers. The Bible says, "...God opposes the proud but gives grace to the humble. (James 4:6 NLT) If the Bible says that God resists the proud, that should be enough ground for any believer to walk in humility at any cost. Because if God should resist a person, who else can they call on for deliverance? There's no one. And pride is when a person insists on their own ways regardless of the will of God.

I love what Samuel said to Saul in 1 Samuel 15:17 (NIV), He said, "You were once small in your own eyes." In other words, you once did not care what others thought of you as long as God was pleased. You were corrected in the house of God and on that account, you took a break from church, isn't that proof that you have not submitted yourself to being disciplined? The truth is that no true pastor would delight in the sadness of those that have been committed to them. However, if the correction of the pastor is needed to deliver you from the jaws of destruction, then it is a necessary sadness that must be borne. Proverbs 3:12 (NLT) says, "For the LORD corrects those He loves, just as a father corrects a child in whom he delights." In other words, correction is a demonstration of the Father's love, and the lack of correction is evidence of a lack of love.

Approach correction and discipline from the standpoint of truth and not emotions. If you are corrected or disciplined, remove your emotions and pride and receive truth and God's love. Discipleship says "I am grateful to God for those who are correcting me in the house of God". Rather than find someone who will agree with your pride and flesh that it was out of place for your pastor to have corrected you. Besides, anyone who is against you being corrected in the house of God is an enemy of your destiny.

The Lord is calling you to submit to discipleship as a lifestyle. Heed God's voice now and live a life of grace upon grace. Hallelujah!

Faith-Filled Confession:
I submit to the discipleship. I stand defenseless to the correction and exhortation of the Word of God and of my spiritual leaders. I accept the love of God for me even when it comes in the form of correction and rebuke.

BE ALERT IN THE SPIRIT AND SPEAK LIFE ONLY

"Be alert and of sober mind. Your enemy the devil prowls around like a roaring lion looking for someone to devour."
(1 Peter 5:8 NIV)

Jesus gave a parable about the kingdom which I believe is instructional in this season of our lives. In this parable, Jesus said, "The Kingdom of Heaven is like a farmer who planted good seed in his field. But that night as the workers slept, his enemy came and planted weeds among the wheat, then slipped away. When the crop began to grow and produce grain, the weeds also grew." (Matthew 13:24,25 NLT) I want you to observe when the enemy came and planted weeds among the wheat; it was when the workers slept. To sleep here means to relax one's hold on the Word. When we do this, we become careless with our speech. An example is when a believer says, "I don't care what the Bible says; I am going to do what I have to do." Mark 4:19 (NIV) describes it as "allowing the worries of this life, the deceitfulness of wealth and the desires for other things to choke the word; making it unfruitful." Not only do we allow these things into our hearts, but ultimately, we let them proceed out of our mouths. The Apostle Paul painted a vivid picture of what it means to let the devil in. Ephesians 4:27 says, "...anger gives a foothold to the devil" and when the devil gets that foothold, he has only one thing on his mind –he sows as many weeds as possible. Weeds here represent unbelief, hopelessness, anger, frustration etc. So, don't be caught off guard. Stay awake!

The Lord is stressing the importance of living a disciplined life, especially in our speech. 1 Peter 5:8 (NIV) says, "Be alert and of sober mind. Your enemy the devil prowls around like a roaring lion looking for someone to devour." I love the way the Message translation puts it. It says, "Keep a cool head. Stay alert. The Devil is poised to pounce and would like nothing better than to catch you napping. Keep your guard up." (1 Peter 5:8 MSG) The only time the devil pounces is when you wander away from the Word; when you give in to negative feelings like unhealthy anger, frustration, and depression. Naptime is when your confessions rebel against the reality of Christ; when you confess fear, inability, weakness, uncertainty, lack, sickness, hopelessness, and everything else that contradicts the life and nature of God in Christ Jesus. Someone asks you, "How are you doing?" And you respond with, "I just hate myself" or "my life is over". Such speech rebels against Christ. Even when it appears as though your life is over, remember this: YOUR LIFE IS NOT OVER. The grace of God is sufficient for you. Pick up what you have left and start all over again. GOD HASN'T WRITTEN YOU OFF. So do not let anyone or the devil for that matter beat you up to the point where you are now confessing death over yourself.

Do not be discouraged. Refuse to meditate on the wrong information even when everything around you suggests that you are alone and that you would not make it out this time. Be alert and consistently speak God's Word because the Word that you speak is sure to prevail in your life.

Faith-Filled Confession:
I refuse to give a foothold to the adversary. I stand my ground on the immovable Word of God. I choose to dwell on the Word. My thoughts are inundated by the Word. I speak the Word only. The Word increases in me and prevails over every circumstance, in Jesus' name, Amen.

CHASTENED BY THE WORD

"For the Lord disciplines those He loves, and He punishes each one He accepts as His child." (Hebrews 12:6 NLT)

Christianity is not a life of popular opinion. It is not according to man's philosophy. It is living according to the Word, and living according to the Word necessitates chastisement. It doesn't matter your position or rank; chastisement is necessary for your growth. So, yes, you are the righteousness of God in Christ Jesus and have been made perfect in Christ Jesus. You may even prophesy and interpret tongues. But you still should expect to be chastened. When this happens, receive it! It is necessary for growth. Hebrews 12:6 says, "For the Lord disciplines those He loves, and He punishes each one He accepts as His child." Read John 15:2.

A fellow once said to me, "Nobody gets my gift and anointing at my church." When I heard those words, I shook my head and recognized that he was going nowhere in life with such an attitude. My greatest concern, however, were those at that church that he had influenced with his attitude. Saints, God is still in the business of resisting the proud. Anyone with such an attitude will resent anyone that corrects them. Proverbs 9:7-9 (NASB) says, "He who corrects a scoffer gets dishonor for himself, and he who reproves a wicked man gets insults for himself. Do not reprove a scoffer, or he will hate you, reprove a wise man, and he will love you. Give instruction to a wise man, and he will be still wiser, teach a righteous man, and he will increase his learning."

Never spiritualize a bad attitude. If someone points out that you have a bad attitude, don't say it is your personality or accuse the person of passing judgment on you. Any personality that does not accentuate godliness is not of God. If your personality sends people away from God, then it is a serious problem. And if you see correction as people getting in your business, you have been deceived by the enemy.

Correction may not always be because you did the wrong thing. Sometimes, you can be corrected because you did the right thing that brought about a negative consequence. This is why 1 Corinthians 8:9 (NIV) says, "Be careful, however, that the exercise of your rights does not become a stumbling block to the weak." In other words, no matter how right you think you are, if your rightness causes your brother to stumble, then you have done no good. Regardless of what prompted the correction, whether it was because you were wrong or because you did the right thing that caused a brother or sister to stumble, receive it with meekness. Each time you receive correction with the right attitude, you receive grace, and your capacity for greater productivity is increased.

Not even Jesus was spared when it came to chastening. Hebrew 5:8 (NLT) says, "Even though Jesus was God's Son, He learned obedience from the things He suffered." In other words, He didn't always get His way. We see this even as He negotiated with the Father in the garden of Gethsemane.

Chastisement is never pleasant to the flesh. It sometimes is soft and private, and other times, it's a stern and public rebuke. Regardless of how it comes, embrace it as a necessity for growth. If you are not corrected by those who should, it means that you are not loved. But if you are chastened, happy, are you! When you receive correction with the right attitude, you can expect promotions to follow.

God bless you.

Faith-Filled Confession:
Henceforth, I receive correction with the right attitude - with gratitude - knowing that God corrects those He loves. Consequently, I am positioned for promotion and increased productivity. In Jesus' name, Amen.

DON'T DELAY YOUR OBEDIENCE

"My Spirit will not put up with humans for such a long time,
for they are only mortal flesh...." (Genesis 6:3 NLT)

Genesis 6:3 NLT says "My Spirit will not put up with humans for such a long time, for they are only mortal flesh..." This tells us that spiritual instructions are time-bound. If God expects for you to act on something and you delay acting, you will miss that opportunity because His call on you is connected to other things and people. If you do not act, He will get someone else that will. Jesus said to the Pharisees, "...if they keep quiet, the stones will cry out." (Luke 19:40 NIV) Because the Pharisees failed to respond to God, others were called upon to take their place, and if those others had failed to respond, the rocks were going to cry out in their place because the work of God must be accomplished. If you are feeling that pull of the Spirit; if God is telling you to get rid of certain habits, behaviors, and tendencies, do it now! Don't try to logically process it. J.ust give in to the demand of the Holy Ghost. I urge you to act quickly before you talk yourself out of a divine invitation of the Spirit.

Imagine if Jesus had allowed His contradictory feelings to take over at the garden of Gethsemane. Had Jesus failed to act on the pruning of the Father to take that next step at the garden of Gethsemane or had He decided to put it off for some other time, do you think we all would be saved today? Certainly not! I believe that Jesus knew that His obedience was time-bound. He had earlier told Peter to pray because something was coming his way. Satan had a plot against Peter's life and Peter had a short window of opportunity to change things. Did Peter pray? No! The Scripture tells us that Peter and the rest of the disciples were very tired. Even when they had a logical reason for not following through with the demand of God, Jesus still said, "Watch and pray that you may not enter into temptation. The spirit indeed is willing, but the flesh is weak" (Matthew 26:41 ESV) Jesus was letting the disciples know that their obedience to prayer was time-bound and that there was no valid excuse for not participating. Praying after taking a nap was not an option either because the instructions of God are time-bound. Praying afterward would have meant operating outside of the spiritual time zone. And such prayer would not have amounted to anything. Jesus said to His disciples, "Are you still sleeping and resting? Look, the hour has come, and the Son of Man is delivered into the hands of sinners." (Matthew 26:45 NIV) Jesus was more or less saying, "Too late now; do not bother about praying anymore." He said, "Rise! Let us go! Here comes my betrayer!" (Matthew 26:26 NIV)

Saints, any delay in obedience will result in disobedience. If Jesus wasn't exempted from God's pruning even when He pleaded with tears, it tells us that the process is non-negotiable with God. Press through the pain because a glorious future awaits you. Give in to the demands of God today, you will not regret it. Let nothing hinder you. Many are dependent on your obedience to God.

Faith-Filled Confession:
I can do all things through Christ who strengthens me. For greater is He that is in me than he that is in the world. I am wise; I make the most of every opportunity that I have to walk in God's destiny and purpose for my life.

PRUNING

"Every branch in Me that does not bear fruit He takes away, and every branch that does bear fruit He prunes, that it may bear more fruit." (John 15:2)

Several years ago, one of my sons said to me, "Pastor, please feel free to correct me whenever I need to be corrected." In other words, he was willingly submitting himself for correction and instruction even before the need arose. Hebrews 12:8 says, "If God doesn't discipline you as He does all of His children, it means that you are illegitimate and are not really His children at all." And in John 15:2, Jesus said, "Every branch in Me that does not bear fruit He takes away..." In other words, anyone who does not submit to the Father's pruning has no part in Jesus. And pruning is critical to the fulfillment of God's plan for our lives.

What is pruning? Pruning is giving in to the demands of God at the expense of your own vision and ideology. Paul the Apostle put it this way in Philippians 3:8: "Indeed, I count everything as loss because of the surpassing worth of knowing Christ Jesus my Lord. For His sake, I have suffered the loss of all things and count them as rubbish, in order that I may gain Christ." In essence, Paul was saying that he gave up his dreams, aspirations, and reputation to see God's will done in his life.

When God prunes, His end goal is your advancement. So think for a moment. When was the last time that God demanded that you make a change in a particular area? And what was your response? If you are one that did not respond in the affirmative, did you notice that things stalled around you due to your failure to act? And when you chose to respond positively, did you also observe the level of peace and how things shifted for your good, spiritually and materially? Whatever your response to God was, it either caused you to move forward with fulfilling God's will for your life, or it caused you to stall or maybe even regress.

So, if things are not going the way you may have anticipated, my charge for you today is that you examine your response to God's pruning. Are you yielding to the corrections of God, or are you resisting them? The bottom line is this: when you offer yourselves to someone as obedient slaves, you are slaves of the one you obey—whether to sin, which leads to death, or to obedience, which leads to righteousness (Romans 6:16). When you yield to God, your life spells out GLORY, but when you resist Him, your life can only spell out darkness, gloom, and doom.

My prayer for you today is that you would attend to the demands of God with joy and that His name would be glorified in you and through you, in Jesus' name. Amen!

Faith-Filled Confession:
The Lord takes delight in me. He rejoices over me with singing and quiets me with His love. I am His beloved child, and my life spells out His G-L-O-R-Y

stewardship

He is calling you, as a steward of His wealth and treasures to be faithful

STEWARDSHIP

"This is how one should regard us, as servants of Christ and stewards of the mysteries of God. Moreover, it is required of stewards that they be found faithful". (1 Corinthians 4:1-2 ESV)

Ephesians 1:11 (GNT) says, "All things are done according to God's plan and decision; and God chose us to be His own people in union with Christ because of His own purpose, based on what He had decided from the very beginning." In other words, there is no one who is alive today that is here to take up space. You are here for a divine assignment; an assignment that God could not entrust to angels or any other being. He uniquely made you based on the assignment He had in mind for you. And with that came the ability, skills, knowledge, wisdom, power, influence, platforms, relationships, opportunities, assets, etc. All of these were given for your effectiveness and for you to fulfill His divine plan for your life.

In the parable of the talents, the Master gave five talents to one, to another, he gave two, to another, he gave one. The Scripture tells us that he gave to each one according to their ability (Matthew 25:14-30). That is to say, that God is the one that decides what our assignment is, not us. He determines the scope and the reach of your call-in life.

In the parable, there was a common understanding of the need for productivity between the Master and his servants. They were required to be faithful stewards of the resources of the Master, just as you and I are required to be faithful stewards of God's resources. The servants were expected to produce more than they had been given. In this parable, the Master's resource to the servants was the talents that they received from him. In your case, it could be your ability, skills, knowledge, wisdom, power, influence, platform, relationships, opportunities, assets, etc. All that God has given to you is for the primary purpose of advancing the agenda of the kingdom of God. You have received all that you have received so that the name of Jesus can be glorified and the gospel advanced.

But if all that you have has advanced your agenda, at the expense of Christ, then you are an unfaithful steward. If you have not taken leverage of that relationship, platform, or opportunity that God has given to you to glorify and advance His gospel, then you are living for yourself just like the servant that did nothing with what He was given. Maybe you have a reason like that servant for why you have not been productive. Or maybe you have allowed fear to keep you from living for God. The Master's response to you will be no different than the Master's response to the servant that was unproductive. He said to him, "...you wicked and slothful servant!" (Matthew 25:26 ESV) In other words, it is wickedness to allow God's treasure in you to go to waste, and there is no acceptable excuse for it. If that response to the unfaithful servant wasn't strong enough, the Master said in verse thirty, "And cast ye the unprofitable servant into outer darkness: there shall be weeping and gnashing of teeth." (KJV)

God takes the things that He has given to us seriously, and He requires for us to be faithful with His resources. For this reason, He is calling you, as a steward of His wealth and treasures, to be faithful. Use all that God has given to you to glorify the name of Jesus and to advance His kingdom in your world, and make the decision to start TODAY.

It is time to account for all that God has given to you.

Faith-Filled Confession:
Father, I thank You for giving me an excellent spirit with which I serve You and those around me. I will serve Your people wholeheartedly and without contempt. Thank You for Your ability that is at work in me, enabling me both to desire and to work out Your good purpose, in Jesus' name, Amen.

STEWARDSHIP EXPRESSED THROUGH SOUL WINNING

"As God's fellow workers, then, we urge you not to receive God's grace in vain." (2 Corinthians 6:1 BSB)

In 1 Corinthians 4:1-2 (BSB), the Bible says, "So then, men ought to regard us as servants of Christ and stewards of the mysteries of God. Now it is required of stewards that they be found faithful." To properly understand this Scripture, one must first understand who a steward is and how faithfulness is measured. In simple terms, a steward is one who acts as a custodian or as a manager. The Bible tells us that we are stewards of the mysteries of God. The question then is, for what purpose? Why did God choose to make us stewards of His mysteries? The answer is simple. He expects for us to take His message to our world. The reason He entrusted us with His mysteries is so that we would share His message with our world and produce more sons and daughters unto Him. 2 Corinthians 5:18 (NKJV) says, just as God "...reconciled us to Himself through Jesus Christ, [He] has given us the ministry of reconciliation." In other words, after you are saved, your primary responsibility is to get others saved. Your heart at every moment should beat for souls to be added to the kingdom of God.

If soul-winning is the primary responsibility of every Christian, why then has it become secondary in many Christian circles today? I believe part of this nonchalant attitude toward soul-winning is because we have heard it said or inferred over, and over again, that the work of Christ is finished. Somehow, we have come to believe that it is not our responsibility anymore to share the gospel with those within our reach. However, when Jesus said, "It is finished," He did not mean that His work was finished. The transaction for salvation was finished but the work of Christ continued even after the resurrection and ascension of Jesus. Apostle Paul writing to the church at Corinth said, "As God's fellow workers, then, we urge you not to receive God's grace in vain." (2 Corinthians 6:1 BSB) Apostle Paul referred to himself and those who were with him as

God's fellow workers. This lets us know that the work of Christ continues, and it continues through us. Then, in 1 Corinthians 9:1 (NKJV), Apostle Paul wrote, "...Are you not my work in the Lord?" Thus, inferring that the Church in Corinth was the fruit of his being a co-laborer with God. Because the Apostle Paul preached the gospel in Corinth and led people to Christ, he could boldly call himself a co-laborer with God, and refer to the people as his work in the Lord.

Saints, we are in the last days, and if there was ever a time when we should be interceding for souls and sharing the gospel, it is now! There is urgency in the spirit. Let us take our place, as faithful stewards, to see to it that souls are added to the kingdom. Then, you can say to the one that you lead to Christ and disciple, "You are the fruit of my work in the Lord."

Faith-Filled Confession:
The Holy Spirit, who lives in me, has equipped me to be an effective soul winner. I am bold to declare the message of Jesus Christ. And I am effective in my ministry of being a reconciler in Jesus' name, Amen.

STEWARDSHIP EXPRESSED THROUGH SERVICE

"Each of you should use whatever gift you have received to serve others, as faithful stewards of God's grace in its various forms." (1 Peter 4:10 NIV)

There is a greater purpose for living than living for one's self, and I dare to say that living for self is not living at all. If your daily, weekly, or monthly calendar is filled with activities that only concern you and your family, you are not living the God-life. God created you for so much more! There is something that He has given to each one of us that He requires for us to use to serve others, and when we serve others in Christ, we ultimately serve God. 1 Peter 4:10 (NIV) says, "Each of you should use whatever gift you have received to serve others, as faithful stewards of God's grace in its various forms." In other words, faithfulness in stewardship is measured in how well you use your God-given abilities to serve God.

Let me ask you, what is it that God has given to you that you could use to serve Him? Could your beautiful voice be a gift that He has given to you for His service? How about your administrative skills? Or could your passion to teach and mentor children be a gift with which you can serve God? God has given to each one of us something that He expects for us to use to serve Him. Romans 12:6-8 (GNT) says, "So we are to use our different gifts in accordance with the grace that God has given us. If our gift is to speak God's message, we should do it according to the faith that we have; if it is to serve, we should serve; if it is to teach, we should teach; if it is to encourage others, we should do so. Whoever shares with others should do it generously; whoever has authority should work hard; whoever shows kindness to others should do it cheerfully."

Child of God, make up your mind, that you will fully put to work your God-given abilities. If you have been sitting on your gifts, now is the time to rise up and do something for God. And if you have been serving God with your God-given abilities in the past,

187

is there more that you can do? Remember that your faithfulness as a steward of Heaven's resources is assessed in how well you utilize all that God has given to you.

Faith-Filled Confession:
I am God's masterpiece, created in Christ Jesus to do good works, which God has prepared in advance for me to do and I will be diligent to do that which He has called me to do.

EVALUATE YOUR STEWARDSHIP (Pt. I)

"This is how one should regard us, as servants of Christ and stewards of the mysteries of God. Moreover, it is required of stewards that they be found faithful." (1 Corinthians 4:1-2 ESV)

There's an old song that says, "Count your blessings, name them one by one, count your blessings and see what God has done. Count your blessings, name them one by one, and it will surprise you what the Lord has done." This song was typically a call to thanksgiving for all that the Lord had done, especially during times when it appeared as though He was far away. As we sang this song, faith in the ability of God was stirred in us. We saw again the miraculous deed of God in our lives, and we sang until the whole congregation busted into spontaneous praise and worship. Looking back now, I can see why some felt like God was a million miles away from them when they needed Him the most. Pastor Chris, a mentor and spiritual father, once said, "You will never experience true fulfillment in God until you are a man or woman on a mission." By this, he was saying that until one functions in the direction in which God has called them, and with the resources entrusted to them, such individuals will feel empty and dissatisfied about life as a whole.

When you recall that God healed you, you should ask yourself how the gospel has advanced since you got healed? Yes, the Lord gave you a promotion on the job, now ask yourself, how has your financial increase helped to advance the work of the Kingdom? The key is not just to count the blessings of the Lord, but to evaluate how you have used His resources as tools to advance His purpose in your world.

Remember that you are a custodian of God's eternal resources on the earth. 2 Corinthians 4:7 (ESV) says, "But we have this treasure in jars of clay, to show that the surpassing power belongs to God and not to us." Therefore, it is an abuse of privilege and access for anyone to use the resources of God for anything other than what God intended. The result of doing so will be a steward that feels empty and dissatisfied. Strangely, when this happens, most stewards want to pray for more resources; not so that they can use it for the service of God, but so that they can continue to live lives that do not give God the glory. James 4:3 (NIV) says, "When you ask, you do not receive, because you ask with wrong motives, that you may spend what you get on your pleasures."

If your desire is to live fulfilled each day, you must evaluate your usage of God's resources. Ask yourself these questions: "How faithful am I in giving my tithes?" "Does the Holy Spirit have liberty in my home?" "Is my body an instrument of righteousness?" "Who has predominant control of my mouth?" "How much time do I dedicate to serving others without expecting anything in return?" The next time you count your blessings, make sure that you are evaluating how your blessings have helped the spread of the gospel in your world.

Faith-Filled Confession:
Thank You Father for Your ability that is at work in me, and for expressing Yourself freely through me. Today, I align myself with your agenda and I show forth your glory, in Jesus' name, Amen.

EVALUATE YOUR STEWARDSHIP (Pt. II)

"This is how one should regard us, as servants of Christ and stewards of the mysteries of God. Moreover, it is required of stewards that they be found faithful." (1 Corinthians 4:1-2 ESV)

Do you desire a life that is full of peace, prosperity, and happiness? If you do, then, you are not alone. Most people desire the same and even more. Many have attended conferences and paid personal coaches to help them achieve these things, yet they still feel dissatisfied with their lives. Some have tried to end one relationship for another, and have moved from one city to another, and it still did not solve the problem. My spiritual father once said, "Whatever you need to be all that God has called you to be is on the inside of you." This thinking changed my life forever. No city, place, or person can determine your destiny in God. Your destiny is in your own hands. However, if you would align yourself with the Spirit of God, you would have a fulfilled destiny.

Child of God, life in Christ is not meant to be filled with frustration, emptiness, and sadness. Success is in you. The solution to enduring peace, prosperity, and happiness lies in you doing the very thing you were anointed to do. Doing otherwise will only amount to frustration and emptiness which is common with the people of the world. Romans 12:6-8 (NKJV) says, "Having then gifts differing according to the grace that is given to us, let us use them: if prophecy, let us prophesy in proportion to our faith; or ministry, let us use it in our ministering; he who teaches, in teaching; he who exhorts, in exhortation; he who gives, with liberality; he who leads, with diligence; he who shows mercy, with cheerfulness." In other words, if you are married, don't desire to be single, and if you are a teacher, don't desire to be a firefighter. Your relevance in life is only achieved when you are in the place of your planting.

Many are committed to things that have no bearing with their destiny. In the parable of the talents, the master did not judge the servant that was given one talent on the account of the ability of the servant that had two talents. Instead, he judged each one according to the ability given to them. It wouldn't have mattered if the servants climbed the highest mountain or built the fastest car. If that was not God's assignment for them, it would have all been in vain. All the Master is concerned about is your faithfulness in what He has called you to do. Someone may say, "But I help the sick and poor even though it's not my calling." Doing a good deed is not good enough; it will never make up for the failure to do God's will. The servant that received one talent did something with it that may have been seen as noble in the eyes of men; yet, he was outside of the master's will. He said to the master, "I was afraid I might disappoint you, so I found a good hiding place and secured your money. Here it is, safe and sound down to the last cent." And the master's response was, "Take the thousand and give it to the one who risked the most. And get rid of this "play-it-safe" who won't go out on a limb. Throw him out into utter darkness."

Child of God, I encourage you to evaluate yourself to determine whether or not you are in God's will for your life because only then can you effectively evaluate your stewardship.

Faith-Filled Confession:
I am set on the path that I must follow. God's will is primary in my life. I refuse to drift or go off course. I will fulfill God's purpose for my life without reproach. Not by power, not by might, but by the Spirit of God, in Jesus' name, Amen

the
gospel

Greater is He that is in me, than he that is in the world
because the tomb is empty

communion

THE TOMB IS EMPTY

"But very early on Sunday morning the women went to the tomb, taking the spices they had prepared. They found that the stone had been rolled away from the entrance. So, they went in, but they didn't find the body of the Lord Jesus." (Luke 24:1-3 NLT)

The key to appropriating the benefit of salvation is to know the significance of the empty tomb. The understanding that Jesus had eternally accomplished the Father's will on your behalf is what I am talking about. Meaning that whatever He did is irreversible and cannot be made void – it is eternally settled. This was the reason He cried out in John 19:30 (NKJV), "IT IS FINISHED!" Therefore, your victory over hell and death is irreversible and your prosperity cannot be made void. Your progress is unstoppable!

These are some of the significance of the empty tomb. In Matthew 8:17 the scripture declares; "HE HIMSELF TOOK OUR INFIRMITIES AND CARRIED AWAY OUR DISEASES." (NASB) Notice that it didn't say, "He is going to take our infirmities when we pray hard enough." Neither did it say, "Our diseases will be carried away if we ask him to." This is something that He took care of even while we were still sinners. The Bible says, "But God, being rich in mercy, because of His great love with which He loved us, even when we were dead in our transgressions, made us alive together with Christ (by grace you have been saved)." (Ephesians 2:4-5 NASB) Until we realize this simple truth, manifesting the significance of why the tomb is empty will be impossible.

Your success is an indication that the tomb is empty in reality. Listen! Your victory is compulsory, without which His resurrection would be without a witness or proof. Understand, your victory was not your idea, it was His! This is why your victory over hell and death is purely based on the reality that the tomb is empty. This is why Romans 8:37 (KJV) declares, "Nay, in all these things we are more than conquerors through Him that loved us." the Amplified put it this way, "Yet amid all these things we are more than conquerors and gain a surpassing victory through Him Who loved us." The next

195

time someone asks you how you know that you are more than a conqueror, just tell them that the tomb is empty. Remember He died because of our offenses, but our justification, health, victory, success, unending progress, peace, prosperity, preservation are all indications that He arose. Just as much as His death was on the account of our sin, so also is our victory and prosperity on the account of His resurrection. This is why praying for victory over any circumstance is absolutely an exercise in futility.

Now that the tomb is empty, impose your victory over every adverse circumstance that may be facing you. They are programmed to yield to your faith proclamations. Live as a king in this world; refuse any kind of misery regardless of what you see and hear. Revelation 1:6 (KJV) declares, "And hath made us kings and priests unto God and His Father; to Him be glory and dominion for ever and ever. Amen." If there is one thing we know about kings, it is the fact that they don't beg. Rather, they make decrees because no word of theirs is void of power. Make up your mind going forward that you will never beg for the significance of the empty tomb, for you have the life, nature and ability of God on the inside of you. Praise God!

Faith-Filled Confession:
Father in the name of the Lord Jesus Christ, I declare that I am more than a conqueror. Greater is He that is in me, than he that is in the world. Because the tomb is empty. I declare that my justification, health, victory, success, unending progress, peace, prosperity, and preservation are unchangeable. I live permanently in divine favor every day. In Jesus name!

TESTIFY OF YOUR SALVATION

"My mouth will tell about Your righteousness, about Your salvation all day long. Even then, it is more than I can understand. I will come with the mighty deeds of the Almighty Lord. I will praise Your righteousness, Yours alone." (Psalm 71:15-16 GWT)

When you look around the world today, you see a lot of hopelessness and pain; many without joy and peace. Many live in fear of the unknown and what is known is sometimes even scarier to them. But thanks be to God that we are no longer of this world! If you are born again, you are not of this world; you have been translated from the kingdom of this world into the kingdom of God (Colossians 1:13). Hallelujah! We are not in despair; neither are we perplexed by the happenings in the world. We have hope, peace and joy! Praise God! We are hope bearers, love extenders and solution givers. We extend the love of Christ to everyone we come across. When we show up, it is with solutions. We have the answer to the cries of many. We bring them the greatest miracle that they could ever have - we bring them ETERNAL LIFE which is in JESUS CHRIST alone.

As Christians, we have the answer that the world needs. No matter the challenge that people are faced with, the answer is JESUS. Outside of Jesus, life will always be chaotic. Only in Him will a person ever experience true love, joy, peace and freedom. He is the only One that satisfies; if you are a Christian, you can attest to this. Simon Peter said, "Lord, to whom would we go? You have the words that give eternal life." (John 6:68 NLT) Jesus said, "Come to me, all you who are weary and burdened, and I will give you rest." (Matthew 11:28 NIV) His invitation is to all. Who will do the job of publicizing His invitation? In the church today, many have relinquished the job of evangelism to the pastors and evangelists. The primary commission of the Christian which is to preach the gospel of Jesus Christ has been neglected. Jesus Himself said, "Go into all the world and preach the gospel to all creation." (Mark 16:15 NIV) And since He gave the command to go, He has not asked for you to return. In other words, this should be your agenda every day that you wake up. The scripture tells us that God is not willing that any should perish, but that all should come to repentance (2 Peter 3:9). Isaiah said, "The Spirit of the Lord is upon me, because the Lord has anointed me; he has sent me to bring good news to the oppressed and to bind up the brokenhearted, to proclaim freedom for the captives, and release from darkness for the prisoners." (Isaiah 61:1 ISV) The reason for the anointing that is on your life is to bring liberation to the lives of those that are bound; the life of that unsaved family member and the life of that unsaved coworker.

You must be bold to testify of your salvation everywhere you find yourself. Testify about how God saved you and invite others to receive the life that you have. Freely you have received, freely give. The Psalmist said, "My mouth will tell about Your righteousness, about Your salvation all day long. Even then, it is more than I can understand. I will come with the mighty deeds of the Almighty Lord. I will praise Your righteousness, Yours alone." (Psalm 71:15-16 GWT) In other words, I will let everyone know that God saved me and that He is still in the business of saving and I will do this with every opportunity I get. He said, I will not only do this with words but I will do this with MIGHTY DEEDS and NOTABLE MIRACLES.

Do not be excited that you are the only one that is saved in your family or at your job. You must have a burden to see people receive salvation. You must have a burden to see a transformation. It is not enough to be a Christian and on your way to Heaven. Who are you taking with you? There is one ministry that every Christian has been called into, and that is the ministry of reconciliation. 2 Corinthians 5:18-19 (NKJV) tells us; "Now all things are of God, who has reconciled us to Himself through Jesus Christ, and has given us the ministry of reconciliation, that is, that God was in Christ reconciling the world to Himself, not imputing their trespasses to them, and has committed to us the word of reconciliation." Today, testify of your salvation and of the Savior, Jesus Christ. Testify of His righteousness which the Bible says, you now are (2 Corinthians 5:21). Testify with your words. Be bold to tell someone about

Jesus and invite them to receive salvation. Testify with your actions. Show love always, even in the face of hate and let your life reflect godliness. Testify with notable miracles. Do not hesitate to pray for people and when you do, expect a miracle! "How beautiful on the mountains are the feet of those who bring good news, who proclaim peace, who bring good tidings, who proclaim salvation, who say to Zion, Your God reigns!" (Isaiah 52:7 NIV)

Faith-Filled Confession:
I testify of the saving power that is in the name of Jesus Christ. I am bold to share the gospel with those in my sphere of influence. I am alive to the ministry of reconciliation. My words and deeds testify of Jesus. The love of God flows through me today. I bring love, peace, joy and hope to those I come across today. In Jesus' name. Amen!

ANSWER YOUR NAME

"For I am not ashamed of the gospel, for it is the power of God for salvation to everyone who believes, to the Jew first and also to the Greek." (Romans 1:16 ESV)

We are living in a season that is so special by every stretch of the imagination. It is a season of grace, prosperity and the manifestation of the Spirit that is producing signs and wonders like we have not experienced before. If you would listen with your spirit, you would hear the sound of miracles hovering over the earth realm. The Spirit of God is saying, "If any would hear and lift their heart to worship, there would be a demonstration of the power of God. Make no mistake about the condition of things (political and economic) as you see them today; these are the fulfillment of prophecies spoken by holy men and women of God in the past. These are the dark days the prophets spoke of and this is only the beginning," saith the Lord. "But in the midst of all these, you must rise with my Word in your mouth; you must rise with boldness from your spirit, for help is not going to come from heaven as many have hoped for. Whatever help is needed is already amongst you." Saith the Lord.

The Lord says, "You my child are the balancing factor. You are my armor, strength and hope to the earth. You carry in your spirit, the solution that they seek; it's my divine presence. I have said, 'you are the light of the world' and these are the days of your shining. Open your spirit to the sound of the heavenly; collapse your being into my Word. Don't conform to the frustration. No! A thousand times no! It is the device of the enemy to put your light out. Others may complain and be frustrated, but you my child MUST NOT! The world around you depends on your light. My Spirit in you is their ecosystem. Listen! I raised you not to conform to their defeat, sickness, hopelessness, hatred and darkness but to be a vehicle of the move of the Spirit. You have conformed for so long. Now I am calling you out. Separate yourself from all that characterize them. Awake to your divine life! Awake to destiny! You are not of this world! Can't you see that?"

"I raised you up together with Christ and to sit together with Him. Why do you talk and act as though you have not been raised to power and glory? Where is my power and glory? Why is the world around you so confused when I have anointed you to be an assembly line of solutions to all their problems? Why is there so much darkness in your cities and why are those around you so impoverished? Where are you my child?" Saith the Spirit of the living God.

I see in my spirit that many have been swayed away by the current condition of things and the Lord is not pleased with it. The death, violence and the economic woes that we see are the result of our negligence to spiritual obligation; our obligation to shine the light of Jesus in our communities and nation as a whole. We as a church in the age of social media and reality entertainment have redefined the intent of faith and prosperity that the Lord has given us. For the most part, we tend to be competing with the world's ways of doing things. Even though the Lord had said in Proverbs 23:17 (NIV) "Do not let your heart envy sinners, but always be zealous for the fear of the LORD." Whatever you have received from the Spirit of God was only given as an outreach tool. Your faith and prosperity were given in order for you to be an effective soul winner. My question for you right now is this, "Are you ashamed to tell someone that you are born again?" If your answer is no, then tell everyone that salvation is made available to them only in Jesus Christ.

Let me remind you of how intense God is concerning the plight of sinners in your world. In Ezekiel 3:18 (NIV), the Lord said and He is saying to you right now, "When I say to a wicked person, 'You will surely die,' and you do not warn them or speak out to dissuade them from their evil ways in order to save their life, that wicked person will die for their sin, and I will hold you accountable for their blood."

Brothers and sisters, wake up to your heavenly obligation. Testify to the world around you that Jesus saves, heals and blesses. Awake to soul-winning! Answer your name.

Faith-Filled Confession:
Father in the name of the Lord Jesus, I say yes to your call to world evangelism, beginning with everyone in my sphere of influence. I ask that you open the eyes of my understanding to my spiritual responsibilities. In Jesus name. Amen.

BEARERS OF GOOD NEWS

"How beautiful upon the mountains are the feet of him who brings good news, who publishes peace, who brings good news of happiness, who publishes salvation, who says to Zion, "Your God reigns." (Isaiah 52:7 ESV)

It's easy to get caught up in one's own world and lose sight of the beautiful life that we have in Christ. It's easy for us to get pre-occupied with who has wronged us and who has treated us unfairly that we lose sight of the reason why we are alive. The challenges that we face are only as big as we have chosen to magnify them. But in the midst of whatever it is that we are faced with, we always have the option to magnify our God and not our problems. The truth is that problems naturally gravitate towards their solution. If you find yourself faced with problems, rejoice! It means that you have the answer! Hallelujah! Do not get so focused on your "issues" that you neglect your spiritual responsibility.

It is your spiritual responsibility as a Christian to bear the good news of Christ. It is your spiritual responsibility to tell the untold about God's amazing grace. It is your responsibility to bring hope to those that are without hope. There is no other way for the message of Christ to go forth. It has to be disseminated through you. The Bible says in Romans 10:13-15 (BSB) "For, everyone who calls on the name of the Lord will be saved. How then can they call on the One in whom they have not believed in? And how can they believe in the One of whom they have not heard? And how can they hear without someone to preach? And how can they preach unless they are sent? As it is written: "How beautiful are the feet of those who bring good news!" The good news is that you have been commissioned and sent by God to do just that! He has sent you forth to preach the gospel to every creature. In Mark 16:15 (NIV), Jesus said, "Go into all the world and preach the gospel to all creation." And till today, He has not asked you to stop. We are still on assignment. Jesus said to His disciples in Acts 1:8 (NKJV), "But you shall receive power when the Holy Spirit has come upon you, and you shall be witnesses to Me in Jerusalem, and in all

Judea and Samaria, and to the end of the earth." Now, we have the Holy Spirit; we have power and we ought to be about sharing the good news of Jesus Christ. The world needs to know that Jesus saves, heals, and delivers and that they no longer have to live in defeat and misery another day of their life.

I love the words of the Spirit through the prophet Isaiah, "How beautiful upon the mountains are the feet of him who brings good news, who publishes peace, who brings good news of happiness, who publishes salvation, who says to Zion, "Your God reigns." (Isaiah 52:7 NKJV) This is our message and this is what we proclaim. So be bold to share the gospel with someone today.

Faith-Filled Confession:
The Holy Spirit, who lives in me, has equipped me to be an effective soul winner. I am bold to declare the message of Jesus Christ. And I am effective in my ministry of being a reconciler in Jesus' name, Amen.

DON'T COMPLICATE THINGS

*"If you preach, just preach God's Message, nothing else;
if you help, just help, don't take over; if you teach, stick
to your teaching; if you give encouraging guidance, be
careful that you don't get bossy; if you're put in charge,
don't manipulate; if you're called to give aid to people in
distress, keep your eyes open and be quick to respond;
if you work with the disadvantaged, don't let yourself get
irritated with them or depressed by them. Keep a smile on
your face." (Romans 12:7-8 MSG)*

To make the most of the grace of God that is upon
our lives, we must continue to focus on the primary agenda of
Heaven. We must devote our energy to a perceived call. We must
learn to do one thing very well and avoid chasing fantasies. Let me
make it plain; trying to get involved in everything out there is a recipe
for frustration and failure. Just because someone did something
and it worked for them doesn't necessarily mean that it will work
for you. It goes back to the syndrome of comparing oneself with
others. This syndrome is what I will credit with the frustration that
you find with many today. If you would only recognize the agenda
of Heaven for your life, and commit to it fully, you and your family
would experience better.

The Apostle Paul said to Timothy, "Do not neglect the gift that is
in you, which was given you through the prophecy spoken over
you at the laying on of the hands of the elders. Be diligent in these
matters and absorbed in them, so that your progress will be evident
to all." (1 Timothy 4:14-15 BSB) In other words, commit without
distractions to your primary goal in life and don't get caught up
with things that have no relationship to your primary goal in life.
Many of us are caught up in a web of activities without real or
clean measurable achievements in life. We often mistake activities
for effectiveness. A person can be active all he or she wants, but
if their activities are not geared towards achieving God's plan and
purposes for their lives, it is all an exercise in futility. God taught
me something that has kept me from having regrets. He said, "Do
not make yourself available to everything or everyone; only make

yourself available to those things and people that are consistent with My plan and purpose for your life."

Too many people spend their valuable time and resources on people and things that do not enhance the quality of their personalities. And for the most part, these things and people have become hindrances to God's plan for their lives. Why would anyone waste his or her life pleasing others at the expense of their God-given purpose? As long as we still have people like this, the graveyard will remain the most expensive real estate in this country. Saints, STOP PLEASING MEN! FOCUS ON YOUR DESTINY! Romans 12:7-8 (MSG) says "If you preach, just preach God's Message, nothing else; if you help, just help, don't take over; if you teach, stick to your teaching; if you give encouraging guidance, be careful that you don't get bossy; if you're put in charge, don't manipulate; if you're called to give aid to people in distress, keep your eyes open and be quick to respond; if you work with the disadvantaged, don't let yourself get irritated with them or depressed by them. Keep a smile on your face." That is to say, don't complicate things; stick with God's agenda for your life. Just keep it simple.

Faith-Filled Confession:
My life is from glory to glory. I do not fail for greater is He that is in me than he that is in the world. I am a victor over hell and darkness. I have overcome this world and all of its systems in Jesus' name, Amen.

victory

Let your every step, smile and word be a message
of Christ's triumph over this world

THE ATTITUDE OF A VICTOR

"I have told you these things, so that in Me you may have [perfect] peace and confidence. In the world you have tribulation and trials and distress and frustration; but be of good cheer [take courage; be confident, certain, undaunted]! For I have overcome the world. [I have deprived it of power to harm you and have conquered it for you]." (John 16:33 AMPC)

When you study scriptures like this, it ought to leave you amazed and in complete awe. Did you notice the contrast it paints? Jesus said in Him you have perfect peace. Meaning, you have prosperity, health, wholeness and tranquility both internal and external. It is not a promise; rather it is a declaration of Truth! Now that you are born again, this is your life! Your life is a place of prosperity and peace! Hallelujah! On the other side, those that are of the world will have and experience tribulation, trials, distress and frustration without a way out. Thank God you are not of the world! (John 15:19)

You may have said this or heard someone say something like this, "If God says I am holy, why is my life such a mess? Why do I experience such chaos in my life?" My response to such a question would be, do you really believe what the Word says? Because if you believe the Word of God, it will make you what it talks about! Listen to me, God will NEVER lie to you. He is not in the business of making men feel good about themselves. Luke 1:37 (ASV) says, "For no word from God shall be void of power." Praise God!

John 10:10 (NLT) Jesus said "...My purpose is to give them a rich and satisfying life." And He already did. Praise God! You ought to be declaring, "I will not accept anything less than that which Jesus died for me to have." But Pastor, I heard the other day on Christian TV, that Christians must suffer persecution. I think I agree; a worry-free life might be a stretch after all."

When the Bible said, "Yea, and all that would live godly in Christ Jesus shall suffer persecution." (2 Timothy 3:12 KJV) It was not referring to a life that undoes what Jesus has already died for you to have. Persecution does not mean a life of sickness, lack, sorrow, hopelessness and frustration. No! Persecution in that verse means that you are being treated wrongly by those who are not saved for living the life that Jesus died for you to have – a life of peace, prosperity and health. The CEB translation puts it this way "In fact, anyone who wants to live a holy life in Christ Jesus will be harassed".

Are there troubles in this world? Absolutely yes! For this reason, Jesus said, "but be of good cheer [take courage; be confident, certain, undaunted]! For I have overcome the world. [I have deprived it of power to harm you and have conquered it for you.]." (John 16:33 AMPC) Meaning, whatever this world is selling, you as a child of God are not buying. We don't participate in their economy of ups and downs. And if they ever show up at your doorstep, have the attitude of a child of God! Do what Jesus did. Use the word and establish your dominion over every circumstance and situation. James said, "Consider it pure joy, my brothers and sisters, whenever you face trials of many kinds." (James 1:2 NIV)

Paul the Apostle said, "And we know that all things work together for good to those who love God, to those who are the called according to His purpose." (Romans 8:28 KJV) Then in 2 Corinthians 4:18 (KJV), the Apostle Paul declared, "While we look not at the things which are seen, but at the things which are not seen: for the things which are seen are temporal; but the things which are not seen are eternal."

Take a look at Caleb and Joshua. When they were faced with the impossible, they declared to the congregation of the children of Israel, "Only rebel not ye against the LORD, neither fear ye the people of the land; for they are bread for us: their defense is departed from them, and the LORD is with us: fear them not." (Numbers 14:9 KJV)

Think victory only because you are a child of the Most High God. Think success. Think possibility. Think ownership. Think surplus. Somebody said some horrible things about you because you are born again, REJOICE!!!!

Faith-Filled Confession:
I am set for life by the Holy Ghost. Christ is my victory today. Come what may, "The Lord is my light and my salvation; whom shall I fear? the Lord is the strength of my life; of whom shall I be afraid? When the wicked, even mine enemies and my foes, came upon me to eat up my flesh, they stumbled and fell." (Psalm 27:1-2 KJV) Hallelujah!

THE TRIUMPHANT YOU

"And in Christ you have been brought to fullness. He is the head over every power and authority." (Colossians 2:10, NIV)

The last thing this world needs is another failure going somewhere to make others failures. The world is already full of people who have PhDs in frustration; you are not here to add to that misery. No! A thousand times no! You may have been told that you were the result of an unfortunate incident or maybe you were abandoned by your birth parents in front of a church; it makes no difference the situation surrounding your birth. Now that you are born again, the scripture declares, "Therefore if any person is [engrafted] in Christ (the Messiah) he is a new creation (a new creature altogether); the old [previous moral and spiritual condition] has passed away. Behold, the fresh and new has come!" 2 Corinthians 5:17 AMPC. Believe the Word, you are different! You may not feel or see it with your optical eyes, but you are so FRESH AND NEW! The situation surrounding your birth no longer has power to determine your future. Hallelujah!

Now that you are born again, you must realize that failure, frustration and murmuring are inconsistent with the life and the nature of God in you. Hear me! Everything about you has been brought to perfection. This means that there is nothing about you that is not first-class. In James 1:18 (AMP), the bible declares that "It was of His own will that He gave us birth [as His children] by the word of truth, so that we would be a kind of firstfruits of His creatures [a prime example of what He created to be set apart to Himself—sanctified, made holy for His divine purposes]." In other words, you are not an accident; you are a child of His desire. Praise God! I love the way the New Living Translation puts it, it reads, "He chose to give birth to us by giving us His true word. And we, out of all creation, became his prized possession." This is to say that Papa God has loved us eternally with the same love with which He loved Jesus. I don't know if you understand it or not, but Papa God does not love Jesus more than He loves you. Thinking about it; it is so amazing! Just to know that God loves you just like He loves Jesus should get the devil running. Hallelujah! It's no wonder the devil can't stand your presence whenever you are thinking, talking and acting the Word. The last person he (devil) wants to see and hear is you. The reason is that everything about you is an emblem of Christ's triumph over his ability. Your presence in this world is a rebuke to his personality. Glory to God!

In Colossians 2:9 the scripture declares to us that "for in Christ all the fullness of the Deity dwells in bodily form." (NIV) In other words, Jesus is the completion of the revelation of the Father and the Holy Ghost. Better still, when you call on the Father, guess who shows up? Jesus! When you call on the Holy Ghost, Jesus also shows up! And it is from this fullness that you were brought forth. This means that you are the result of the fullness of God in the person of Jesus. You came out of His fullness, wired to display that same fullness from which you were born. This is why I have always said that nothing about you is subject to defeat and failure. Then it says this in the tenth verse of the same chapter that, "in Christ you have been brought to fullness. He is the head over every power and authority." Meaning, it was a triumphant personality that Papa God gave birth to; not a beggarly and weak personality. Papa God did not give birth to a personality that is subject to sickness and misery. No! Not even the devil is a match.

No wonder Paul declares by the Holy Ghost in 2 Corinthians 2:14 (AMPC) "... thanks be to God, who in Christ always leads us in triumph [as trophies of Christ's victory] and through us spreads and makes evident the fragrance of the knowledge of God everywhere." Hallelujah! Your triumph over lack, sickness and every demon hatched out of hell is perpetual. It has no expiration date. Let this be your meditation today. Let this truth flood your soul. Confess it with gusto that you are victorious over sickness, misery and anything that contradicts what grace has made available to you in Christ. Declare that you have gained a surpassing victory already. Praise God!

Faith-Filled Confession:
I live triumphing over frustration, bitterness, wickedness, lack, division and all the works of Satan and the flesh. I rule over this world in and by the anointing of the Holy Spirit. I have gained a surpassing victory over all that is called failure. In the name of the Lord Jesus Christ. I refuse to beg, cry or be in despair because the Lord is my every present help. And He has supplied all that I require to live a life of glory today. Praise God!

UNSHAKABLE ATTITUDE

"Therefore, my dear brothers and sisters, stand firm. Let nothing move you. Always give yourselves fully to the work of the Lord, because you know that your labor in the Lord is not in vain". (1 Corinthians 15:58 NIV)

Having an unshakable attitude on the integrity of the Word of God is not a suggestion from the Spirit of God; it's a requirement to living in the fullness of the blessings of Christ. Too many are not living the victorious life that is in Christ Jesus and it ought not to be so. Victory over lust and lack should not be a big deal to the church; they are 'pre-fundamentals' of the Christian faith. The fact that it has taken the center stage in the life of so many should tell us something. Listen! As long as Satan can preoccupy an individual with things that they ought not to be preoccupied with in the first place like lust, lack, anger, impaired self-esteem, sickness and demonic oppression means that such individual would never walk in the greater glory of the Spirit. Please hear me! Everything that has to do with provision, prosperity, health and victory over the darkness that exists in this world was dealt to you the day you got saved. Meaning, you were given just one task at salvation; ENJOY ALL THINGS. 1 Timothy 6:17 (NLT) says, "Teach those who are rich in this world not to be proud and not to trust in their money, which is so unreliable. Their trust should be in God, who richly gives us all we need for our enjoyment."

I can't overemphasize this enough: stop trying to get victory. Be victorious on every count. Stop trying to live the Christian life from the standpoint of the senses. Your victory over the world, flesh and Satan is not a subject that is up for discussion in the realm of the spirit. It's a matter that cannot be brought to the floor in the court of the Father in heaven for debate. Everything that came to you as a result of your salvation is eternal. They will not, cannot, do not pass the test for discussion. Your provision, prosperity and triumph over hell and death are FOREVER SETTLED. Can this be your attitude? A while ago, the Lord said something to me that really blessed me. He said, "Son, you have more than enough to get more than you need; look in your spirit." In other words, there is nothing that pertains to living each day in absolute victory in this world, financially and otherwise, that is not already on the inside of you. Then He said, "Make no mistake son, you are more than a conqueror. Be strong and very courageous." Hallelujah! And my response was, "Yes Sir! I am strong and very courageous; I refuse to flinch in the face of contrary situations." Hallelujah!

I believe the Lord is saying to you right now, be strong in the grace that is in Christ Jesus. In other words, take advantage of the grace of God that is on you. Be beautiful in all respects; let your body language be a prophetic tool. Let your every step, smile and word be a message of Christ's triumph over this world. Don't give in to religion and half-baked revelation. Stand firm! Let nothing move you. "...Always give yourselves fully to the work of the Lord, because you know that your labor in the Lord is not in vain." (1 Corinthians 15:58 NIV) Brothers and sisters, your faith filled confessions are not for nothing. Ecclesiastes 11:3 (KJV) says, "If the clouds be full of rain, they empty themselves upon the earth..." This means that your giving and confessions are not for nothing. They are seeds for the future that have the ability to alter the picture of today.

Therefore, be unmovable when it comes to your finances after you must have given and done what the Lord asked of you. Be unshakable when your body is speaking a language other than divine health. Use your faith confession to compel your world to line up with His Word. Have an unshakable attitude, knowing that you are a victor already. Praise God!

Faith-Filled Confession:
My mind is made up concerning His Word today. Impossible is nothing with my God. I see a victorious and prosperous me. I refuse any contrary picture of me that does not depict Christ's eternal triumph over hell and death. No matter what I see, feel or hear. I am more than a conqueror. Therefore, I live as a king today. In the name of the Lord Jesus Christ. Hallelujah!

IT'S ALL IN YOUR MOUTH

"For with the heart men believe and obtain righteousness, and with the mouth they make confession and obtain salvation." (Romans 10:10 Weymouth New Testament)

Do you realize that you cannot live right until you start to talk right? Many want to live right while they maintain a wrong confession, and that will not work! You cannot walk in victory until you consistently declare that you are a victor in Christ Jesus. Talking right means that your confessions agree with all that Jesus died for you to have. It is speaking the language of God; it is speaking the Word. It may not be factual in human eyes, but if God said so, then it must become your reality.

In Genesis 3, after Adam and his wife had eaten of the forbidden fruit and discovered that they were naked, "...the Lord God called to the man, 'Where are you?' He replied, 'I heard you walking in the garden, so I hid. I was afraid because I was naked." (Genesis 3:10 NKJV) And God said to Adam, "Who told you that you were naked?" In essence, God was saying, "Adam you are not talking right. Who have you been listening to? Your words are inconsistent with divine reality." Factually, Adam was naked, but he didn't know that he was naked until he ate from the forbidden tree. The forbidden tree here represents the world and her way of doing things. Therefore, when Adam ate the fruit of that tree, he exchanged the supernatural for the natural. That same moment, his confession changed and so did his life. This is the same situation with many of God's people today. Their talking is wrong. They speak a strange language that is not consistent with the Word of God. You hear Christians confessing depression, lack, sickness, bitterness and the list goes on. They do this thinking that they are just being humble and sincere or simply stating the facts. What they fail to realize is that the darkness (depression, sickness, lack etc.) is their creation.

As a Christian, you cannot live above or beyond your confessions. You are the result of what you have said and continue to say. As long as you are confessing depression, bitterness, and lack, you will never enjoy increase. It makes no difference how much you earn or how much you have in your bank account. It will be just a matter of time before lack and poverty eventually seize you as their possession. Because ultimately, what you say, is what you become. It's a law of the spirit.

Saints, let no one deceive you. Your confession is responsible for the condition of things. Not the devil but what you say. God said to the children of Israel "So tell them, 'As surely as I live, declares the Lord, I will do to you the very thing I heard you say." (Numbers 14:28 NIV) I remember getting on an elevator and there was a fellow on the elevator who volunteered to punch the button for everyone. He asked me, "Are you going down?" I simply said, "No! Please, do you mind pressing the G button?" Listen, He was a nice guy and I appreciated his gesture, but I was mindful of success and increase. I was not going to allow anyone to hem me into agreeing with something I knew was contrary to the word of God for my life. Jesus said, "Again I say unto you, that if two of you shall agree on earth as touching anything...." (Matthew 18:19 KJV) I knew I had to disagree with the fellow.

Child of God, the Word is in your heart and in your mouth, so appropriate the glory of it with your confession. Refuse to think or speak contrary to the glory of God for your life. Don't accept the natural as your reality. You are supernatural all the way. Dictate to your situation how it's going to turn out.

Faith-Filled Confession:
No matter the situation, I do not go down. Irrespective of the contrary wind of life, I have the victory in all circumstances. I have increase in all directions. My success is not subject to debate. It is eternally settled. In the name of the Lord Jesus Christ. Amen

IT WILL COME INTO BEING

"If you remain in Me and My words remain in you, ask whatever you wish, and it will be done for you." (John 15:7, Berean Study Bible)

Believing in the words of Jesus is the secret to a life of peace and plenty. I know that some people don't believe that we can live every day in absolute peace, victory and plenty. But the words of Jesus are eternally settled, and the default state of every child of God is that of absolute peace, victory and plenty. Remember Jesus' words in John 10:10, "The thief's purpose is to steal and kill and destroy. My purpose is to give them a rich and satisfying life." (NLT) This rich and satisfying life was already made available to us at salvation. Hence, every child of God now has a rich and satisfying life.

That the truth is not evident in the life of an individual, does not in any way make it less of the truth. It is your responsibility for your life to mirror the eternal victory of Jesus. Jesus has done all that was needed for you to live your best lives now, it's now your turn to live that life to the praise of His name.

I'll say it again; you must believe the Word for you to enjoy the life of God that is in you. You must believe it not as a religious person but as a child. Children don't know enough to doubt a promise. They believe anything that is said to them and they act upon their belief. They believe it so much that they start sharing it with friends. You hear them tell their friends about their plans to go on a vacation, even though when you said it, you didn't really mean it. You only said it so that they could act right. But kids don't know the difference. They believe it anyway. The good news is that God's Word is sure. Every word that He speaks to you is already settled. He means every word that He says. Hebrews 6:17-18 says, "So when God wanted to make the unchanging nature of His purpose very clear to the heirs of the promise, He guaranteed it with an oath. Thus, by two unchangeable things in which it is impossible for God to lie...." (Berean Study Bible)

In the light of the unchanging nature of the Word, let's look again at Jesus' words in John 15:7 and I want you to believe this with your life because it will put you over in every situation. Jesus said, "If you remain in Me and My words remain in you, ask whatever you wish, and it will be done for you." (ESV) This puts so much power in your hands! Jesus said, "...ask whatever you wish," not whatever God desires but whatever you desire. And when you ask, Jesus said it will be done. And the Greek Word for done, ginomai means to come into being. In other words, God doesn't have to do anything for this to happen. Jesus is saying if you remain in Him and His Word remains in you, whatever you say will leap into existence. But the key here is fellowship. Whatever you say from the place of intimacy with Jesus carries creative power that will cause things to come into being just like we saw with God the Father in the Book of Genesis.

Child of God, you have all that you require to live a life of absolute peace, victory and plenty. My prayer today is that this world will come to an understanding that there is a God in you even as you manifest His glory.

Faith-Filled Confession:
The grace, favor, and spiritual blessing of the Lord Jesus Christ; the love of God, and the presence and fellowship, communion, sharing together, and participation in the Holy Spirit is with me today and forever. Amen

LOOK BEYOND AND LAUGH

"Thou wilt shew me the path of life: in thy presence is fullness of joy; at thy right hand, there are pleasures forevermore." (Psalm 16:11 KJV)

No one, not even the devil, can give you a bad day. Psalm 118:24 (NKJV) says, "This is the day the Lord has made. We will rejoice and be glad in it." In other words, no matter the circumstances that arise each day, we are expected to remain glad and joyful. This is God's will concerning you.

A fellow once said, "Everything was okay until someone showed up." But the truth is that if he was really having a great day that was rooted in the Word, nothing would have been able to change it. Jesus put it this way: "Everyone then who hears these words of Mine and does them will be like a wise man who built his house on the rock. And the rain fell, and the floods came, and the winds blew and beat on that house, but it did not fall, because it had been founded on the rock. And everyone who hears these words of Mine and does not do them will be like a foolish man who built his house on the sand. And the rain fell, and the floods came, and the winds blew and beat against that house, and it fell, and great was the fall of it." (Matthew 7:24-27 ESV)

The one that built his house on the sand can be likened to the fellow who was having a great day until he was faced with a challenge. The challenge was able to change his experience because he was not operating his day according to the Word. Now, someone may ask, "What if someone lost a job, house, car, or a multibillion-dollar deal, are they still expected to stay joyful?" The answer is a resounding YES! When your day is rooted in the Word, none of these things can change it. If you are truly conducting your day by the Word and through the guidance of the Holy Spirit, your only response to the loss of a house, car, job, or billion-dollar deal would be to rejoice! James 1:2 (NIV) says, "Consider it pure joy, my brothers and sisters, whenever you face trials of many kinds." Hallelujah! In other words, give no room for despair, sadness, or defeat. No matter what comes your way, consider it pure joy.

221

David said in Psalm 16:11 (KJV), "Thou wilt shew me the path of life: in thy presence is fullness of joy; at thy right hand there are pleasures forevermore." Saint, this is your life; you live in God's presence 24/7, and in His presence is fullness of joy, and at His right hand are pleasures forevermore. So, look beyond whatever imperfection that the day may bring and declare that your life is full of joy and peace. Look beyond and see God working in you and rejoice because victory is your name. Declare that this day is one of strength and beauty in Jesus' name.

Faith-Filled Confession:
I'll sing praises to the Lord, for He is God. I will exalt His name forever. The Lord is the source of all my joy; I will praise Him with all that I am. He has made known to me the path of life. In His presence, I have fullness of joy at His right hand, I enjoy pleasures forevermore. Hallelujah!

blessing

The manifestation of the blessing is made possible
only when you operate by faith; that is, faith in the Word

Communion

MANIFESTING THE BLESSING

"The lines are fallen unto me in pleasant places; yea, I have a goodly heritage." (Psalm 16:6 KJV)

As a Christian, you have the advantage in life. You have been called into a life of glory and splendor. Your godly heritage makes you different from the rest of the world. You were begotten of God and because of your birth; all that the Father has is yours. You were not born into the kingdom of God to suffer again. The Bible says that you were called to inherit a blessing (1 Peter 3:9). David was so confident about the life of the righteous, that he said in Psalm 23:1 (NIV), "The Lord is my shepherd, I lack nothing." You lack nothing! For Christ is your sufficiency! Hallelujah! You do not lack in health, finances, wisdom, inspiration, strength or abilities. You have more than enough. Glory to God!

Ephesians 1:3 (NIV) says, "Praise the God and Father of our Lord Jesus Christ! Through Christ, God has blessed us with every spiritual blessing that heaven has to offer." Child of God, you have been blessed with every blessing that heaven has to offer! But there is something you must know about the blessing. The blessing in itself is not an object. The blessing is not the job, house, car, or money. The blessing is an empowerment; an anointing that causes you to manifest the job, house, car, money, etc. So, it is possible to see one who is blessed manifesting lack. This is possible if the one who is blessed is ignorant of what the blessing is or opposes the working of the blessing in his/her life.

Psalm 1 gives us insight into how this can happen. It says, "Blessed is the man who walks not in the counsel of the ungodly, nor stands in the path of sinners, nor sits in the seat of the scornful, but his delight is in the law of the Lord, and in His law, he meditates day and night. He shall be like a tree planted by the rivers of water, that brings forth its fruit in its season, whose leaf also shall not wither; and whatever he does shall prosper." (Psalm 1:1-3 NKJV) So, even though it is true that God has blessed us with all that we would ever need in life, certain principles must be observed in order for the blessing to be manifested.

For example, to manifest the blessing, one must become a habitual doer or practitioner of God's Word. James 1:22-25 (NKJV) tells us, "But be doers of the Word, and not hearers only, deceiving yourselves. For if anyone is a hearer of the Word and not a doer, he is like a man observing his natural face in a mirror; for he observes himself, goes away, and immediately forgets what kind of man he was. But he who looks into the perfect law of liberty and continues in it and is not a forgetful hearer but a doer of the work, this one will be blessed in what he does." So, it is in the doing of the Word that the blessing is made manifest. Psalms 1:3 (NKJV) has a beautiful description of such a person, who has given themselves wholeheartedly to the Word of God. It says that such a person will be "like a tree planted by the rivers of water that brings forth its fruit in its season, whose leaf also shall not wither; and whatever he does shall prosper."

So get to the Word and walk in the light of it.

Faith-Filled Confession:
The lines have fallen unto me in pleasant places. I am mightily blessed of God. I am not disadvantaged in any way. I set my gaze on the Word of God. I showcase the blessing in my life. I manifest health, wealth, productivity, tranquillity, abilities, opportunities and unending increase! In Jesus' name. Amen.

THE BLESSING IS IN GIVING

"In everything I did, I showed you that by this kind of hard work we must help the weak, remembering the words the Lord Jesus Himself said: 'It is more blessed to give than to receive.'" (Acts 20:35 NIV)

Many of God's people are more inclined and more excited to receive than they are to give. I am yet to meet someone that got upset over receiving. In fact, in most churches today, there is a palpable consciousness of receiving, with hardly any consciousness of giving. Yet, when you study the scriptures, giving precedes receiving. So, one can wait all day expecting to receive, but until there first is giving, their wait would endless. Genesis 8:22 (KJV) says, "While the earth remaineth, seedtime and harvest, and cold and heat, and summer and winter, and day and night shall not cease." In Galatians 6:7 (NLT), Paul the Apostle said, "Don't be misled—you cannot mock the justice of God. You will always harvest what you plant." The one who sowed nothing will also reap nothing, no matter how long he/she spends praying. Financial seeds beget financial harvest. You will only get what you first planted.

2 Corinthians 9:7 (AMPC) says, "...God loves (He takes pleasure in, prizes above other things, and is unwilling to abandon or to do without) a cheerful (joyous, prompt to do it") giver [whose heart is in his giving]." The one who God prizes above others and is unwilling to do without is not the receiver, but a cheerful giver. Then the next verse tells us just what God will do for the giver. It says, "And God is able to make all grace (every favor and earthly blessing) come to you in abundance, so that you may always and under all circumstances and whatever the need be self-sufficient [possessing enough to require no aid or support and furnished in abundance for every good work and charitable donation]." (2 Corinthians 9:8 AMPC) In other words, while the non-giver experiences lack, the giver will enjoy prosperity and abundance; requiring no aid or support.

A giver is never at a disadvantage; regardless of the prevailing circumstance. Jesus said in Acts 20:35 (KJV), "...it is more blessed to give than to receive." Giving is the way of life for the believer and the blessing is made manifest in the life of a giving believer. The more you give, the more you will have to give; generosity begets generosity. So, I want to challenge you to look out for a need in your church in the lives of those around you and meet it. Be generous to someone on the job. Be generous to a stranger. Ask yourself this question: "What can I do to lift someone up today?" What can I give that will make God smile today? Remember that the little things of this life make the biggest impact. Since you have the nature of your heavenly Father, let His nature be seen in you today.

Faith-Filled Confession:
I am a channel of God's love and grace to those around me. I will not hoard or hold back the blessings of God. Even as I have been blessed, I will bless others.

NO MORE

"For all who have entered into God's rest have rested from their labors, just as God did after creating the world."
(Hebrews 4:10 NLT)

I have said repeatedly, and I will say it again, that suffering is inconsistent with the Christian life. It is disturbing to know that many of God's people see it as something holy and part of the Christian experience. The only suffering the Bible tells us to expect as Christians is the persecution that comes on account of our faith (Matthew 5:11); not being sick, living in confusion or lacking the basic resources required for living. No Christian should live another day in sickness or lacking the basic resources required for living an excellent and buoyant life. It is inconsistent with the life of God. Light and darkness cannot co-exist. And if God is not a man that He should lie, you have no business living a life that is void of prosperity and wholesomeness. Jesus' death was not in vain. He brought you into oneness with the Father, and now that you are one with Him, you ought to be a wonder to your world! Let your life be colored with prosperity, humility and grace.

The Spirit of the Lord said to me, "Say to My children, "LABOR NO MORE BECAUSE YOU ARE IN MY REST." You do not have to labor to enjoy wealth, health victory, dominion and peace. These are experiences that are available to you because of Jesus' life, death, resurrection, and ascension. They are expressions of the God-life that you have. They are inherent benefits of being in Christ and do not require you to work to earn them. The price has already been paid by Jesus. All you have to do is to acknowledge that they are part of the package and confess it to be so. Jesus said, "Therefore do not worry, saying, 'What shall we eat?' or 'What shall we drink?' or 'What shall we wear?' For the pagans pursue all these things, and your Heavenly Father knows that you need them. But seek first the kingdom of God and His righteousness, and all these things will be added unto you." (Matthew 6:31-33 NKJV) And now that you are in this kingdom,..." all things are yours. whether Paul or

Apollos or Cephas or the world or life or death or the present or the future. All of them belong to you." (1 Corinthians 3:21-22 BSB)

Stop laboring for what you already have. Open your heart to the visions of the Spirit. Let the Word dominate your spirit. Live in the Word. Acknowledge and confess that you have God's divine ability at work in you. Don't confess lack, inability or insufficiency. Declare like the Apostle Paul, "I am self-sufficient in Christ's sufficiency; I am ready for anything and equal to anything through Him who infuses me with inner strength and confident peace." (Philippians 4:13 AMP) Declare that you walk in wisdom, make wise decisions, and produce excellent results.

Faith-Filled Confession:
I declare that I have entered the rest of God. I have ceased from my labor and now, I enjoy health, peace, and prosperity. The Spirit of God strengthens me, and I have God's divine ability at work in me, making me record supernatural accomplishments. In Jesus' name. Amen.

FAITH IN THE BLESSING

"I will make you into a great nation, and I will bless you; I will make your name great, and you will be a blessing." *(Genesis 12:2 ESV)*

The manifestation of the blessing is made possible only when you operate by faith; that is, faith in the Word. The blessing will not be made manifest, as long as you look at physical entities to determine its authenticity. Do you realize that getting a new house is not evidence that one is blessed? The proof that you are blessed is not in the new house but in the Word. And until you operate with that consciousness, your experiences will not reflect what the Word says. I remember hearing a fellow once said, "If I am blessed, why then are things so unpleasant?" Sadly, he is not alone in this way of thinking; so many of God's people function this way. Hear me saints, your experiences, good or bad, do not validate the Word of God. God's Word is independent of every situation. The Word of God needs no validation from anything or anyone because the Word is God. It does not matter that things appear to be unpleasant right now; it does not in any way change the reality that you are who God says you are.

David said something remarkable in Psalm 37:25 (NIV). He said, "I was young and now I am old, yet I have never seen the righteous forsaken or their children begging bread." In this scripture, David was alluding to God's faithfulness to the righteous and not so much the experiences of the righteous. Saint, God is faithful. If the Word says that you have been blessed, do not try to mentally analyze it. See and address yourself that way, irrespective of whether your experiences/current position reflects it or not. 2 Corinthians 4:18 KJV) says "While we look not at the things which are seen, but at the things which are not seen; for the things which are seen are temporal, but the things which are not seen are eternal." In other words, pay no attention to things that you can discern with your senses. You are to look at those things which are not seen; focus on unseen realities in God's Word. So that fellow, who questioned whether he was blessed or not, based on transient circumstances of life, was looking at the wrong thing.

Hear me, saint! You are a blessing. Have faith in it! Things may not look like you are a blessing right now, but don't be alarmed. Circumstances and situations are subject to change. The only thing that will not change is the reality that God has made you a blessing - a reservoir of eternal resources in the earth realm. You are not just blessed you are more than blessed – you are a blessing! So have faith in it and walk with the consciousness that you are a blessing to your world. You are a gift from God, and an asset from heaven to bless your world. So, allow your words and conduct to reflect who you are - a blessing. This is your call saints; it's a call to bless everyone in your world with the blessings of Christ. Hallelujah!

Faith-Filled Confession:
I was called to inherit a blessing. Right now, I possess the blessing. It does not matter the transient circumstances of life. I AM A BLESSING. No matter what I may see, hear or feel, I AM A BLESSING. Everywhere that I go, I manifest the blessing. Everything I touch is blessed; everyone I come in contact with comes in contact with the blessing of God. This is God's word and it is my consciousness. Hallelujah!

ENFORCE THE BLESSING WITH PROPHECY

"Timothy, my child, I entrust to you this command, which is in accordance with the words of prophecy spoken in the past about you. Use those words as weapons in order to fight well." (1 Timothy 1:18 GNB)

Nothing just happens. There is no such thing as, "I don't know how it happened." Hebrews 11:3 (KJV) says "Through faith, we understand that the worlds were framed by the Word of God so that things which are seen were not made of things which do appear." In other words, the elders, by faith, fashioned, repaired, and mended the course of their life with the Word of God. When things appeared not to be going the way that they believed God had ordered, rather than cry and throw in the towel, they took a hold of the Word. They proclaimed the Word, over, and over again, until it gained dominion over their circumstances.

We have the authority to fashion our course of life in the earth; that authority has been given to us by God. So, don't expect Him to do something about a situation that He has equipped you to handle. You have the power to frame and to change the course of your life. God has given you His Word as it relates to your affairs in this life (health, finances, family, job, etc.). Now, it's up to you to either frame it in accordance with the revealed truth or with something else. Remember what He told Moses in Exodus 25:40 (NIV). He said to him, "See that you make them according to the pattern shown you on the mountain." In other words, I have shown you what it should be, so go and build it per the blueprint; frame it to be so! Praise God!

Things may appear gloomy right now; it may look like it's all but over. But cheer up! It doesn't matter what the situation may be; be it homelessness, physical, or financial challenge, there is good news! And the good news is that you can prophesy yourself out of the dilemma into God's glorious destiny for your life. It's not about what happens to us; it is about what we do with what happens, for in the latter lies our testimony. Speaking rebellious words will do no good but drive you off the cliff in no time. And if that has already happened, with prophecy, you still can bring yourself to your destined place in God.

As earlier mentioned, you must reject the tendency to speak rebellious words - words, which do not take into account the person and the ministry of Jesus. "My life is over"; "I am in a very dark place right now", such words do not recognize the ministry of Jesus in your life. Rather than speak in rebellion, choose to enforce the blessings of God over your life. No matter what you feel, see, or hear, refuse to speak forth your situation. Only speak the Word of God. Prophesy your way out of trouble. Enforce the blessing; compel the material to conform to the reality of the Spirit of God for your life.

Say this with me, "I refuse to live a pitiful life. My life is Christ. I am victorious, exquisite, and perfected in Christ Jesus." Wherever you find yourself, rejoice and refuse to carry a sorry, broken, and defeated demeanor. Matthew 12:37 (NLT) says "The words you say will either acquit you or condemn you." Not only does your life depend on what you say, but those around you can also suffer the collateral effect of your negative words. So, pay attention to what you say and see to it that your words reflect the future that you desire. If you desire prosperity, then prophesy prosperity. Use your words to color your future. It's all in your mouth. Your glorious future and well-being lie in your mouth. So, use your mouth to enforce the blessings of God for your life.

Faith-Filled Confession:
I refuse to live a pitiful life. My life is Christ. I am victorious, exquisite, and perfected in Christ Jesus. All things work together for my good. The joy of the Lord is my strength. I live the blessed life in the here and now. In the name of my Lord and Savior, Jesus Christ, Amen.

THANK GOD FOR HIS BLESSINGS

"All praise to God, the Father of our Lord Jesus Christ, who has blessed us with every spiritual blessing in the heavenly realms because we are united with Christ." (Ephesians 1:3 NLT)

What you see in the physical is not all that there is to any given matter. There is a greater realm called the spiritual realm that controls what you experience in the physical realm. In fact, the physical only exists because of the spiritual. You do not have to accept all that you see in the physical. As a believer in Jesus Christ, you must be cognizant of what exists in the spiritual realm, so that when you notice things that are contrary happening in the physical, you can enforce what you see in the spiritual realm. The spiritual realm is a greater realm and this is where you ought to live from. 2 Corinthians 4:18 (KJV) says, "While we look not at the things which are seen, but at the things which are not seen: for the things which are seen are temporal; but the things which are not seen are eternal." While the physical realm houses temporal things that are subject to change, the spiritual realm holds eternal realities, upon which we must set our gaze.

These unseen realities exist in God's Word. Therefore, we must keep our gaze on the Word of God. You may currently be physically in a situation that does not look favorable; still, rejoice! For it has come to pass. Hallelujah! The unseen reality remains that you are more than a conqueror (Romans 8:37). You may have been diagnosed with one illness or the other. Let me remind you that it is only in the physical realm that the diagnosis exists. So, rejoice! It does not change the unseen reality that by His stripes you were (past tense) healed! (1 Peter 2:24). You may feel alone and neglected. It does not change the eternal reality that you are never alone. For He (God) has said, "I will never leave you nor forsake you." (Hebrews 23:5 NIV)

No matter how you may feel today, the eternal reality remains that you are blessed. You may not feel blessed, you may not look blessed, and may not even smell blessed but all of that is physical and subject to change. Ephesians 1:3 (NLT) declares, "All praise to God, the Father of our Lord Jesus Christ, who has blessed us with every spiritual blessing in the heavenly realms because we are united with Christ." In the spiritual realm you are blessed and to be blessed means that you have been empowered to prosper! Not only financially but in all facets of life. Hallelujah! You are blessed with wisdom, blessed in your health, finances, business, relationships, and every area of your life. Glory to God! 2 Peter 1:3 (NIV) puts it this way; "His divine power has given us everything we need for a godly life through our knowledge of Him who called us by His own glory and goodness." In other words, everything that is required for you to be successful here on earth has already been given to you and currently exists in the realm of the spirit. How then do you make the withdrawal? The answer lies in 2 Peter 1:3. It is through our knowledge of Him. The Greek Word for knowledge in that scripture is 'epignosis'. It means a knowledge that comes from recognition and discernment. If we do not recognize that this scripture is our reality or are unable to discern that it applies to us today and to every facet of living, then, we cannot enjoy to the fullest all that we have been blessed with. Any prayer by a Christian that is asking for God to bless is a prayer that is prayed amiss. For God has already blessed us not with some but ALL spiritual blessings. Our response should be to recognize what is ours and endorse it to be so. Rather than pray, "Bless me, Father God." Say, "I Thank you, Father, for blessing me with all that I require to live a victorious life and I proclaim your blessing in all that I do." That is a prayer that heaven will rejoice over and will cause angels to be dispatched to ensure that you experience all that comes with being blessed. Praise God!

Faith-Filled Confession:
I am blessed with all that I require to live victoriously on the earth. I refuse to live short of all that God has for me. The lines have fallen to me in pleasant places; doors of opportunities open up to me because I am blessed and favored of God. Today, I keep my gaze on the eternal realities in God's Word. I proclaim that I am blessed, prosperous, strong, wise, peaceful and joyful In Jesus' name. Amen.

ABOUT THE AUTHOR

Emmanuel is the president of CHARIS MINISTRIES and the senior pastor of an ever-expanding Grace House Church, with campuses in Canada, Nigeria, and the United States. He is a well-known Bible teacher, author, a member of the John Maxwell Coaching Team, and a conference speaker. He hosts monthly healing meetings that have brought restoration and salvation to many. Pastor E, as he is fondly called, teaches believers everywhere of their inherent right and ability to live the glorious life that they have in Christ Jesus. One of his favorite phrases is that "every believer is called to get the hell out of peoples' lives." This is his first devotional book—a classic on the new creation reality and the authority of the believer.

CPSIA information can be obtained
at www.ICGtesting.com
Printed in the USA
BVHW071059030621
608731BV00002B/185